S. Hrg. 114–638

EXPLORING AUGMENTED REALITY

HEARING

BEFORE THE

COMMITTEE ON COMMERCE, SCIENCE, AND TRANSPORTATION UNITED STATES SENATE

ONE HUNDRED FOURTEENTH CONGRESS

SECOND SESSION

NOVEMBER 16, 2016

Printed for the use of the Committee on Commerce, Science, and Transportation

U.S. GOVERNMENT PUBLISHING OFFICE

25–407 PDF   WASHINGTON : 2017

For sale by the Superintendent of Documents, U.S. Government Publishing Office
Internet: bookstore.gpo.gov   Phone: toll free (866) 512–1800; DC area (202) 512–1800
Fax: (202) 512–2104   Mail: Stop IDCC, Washington, DC 20402–0001

(II)

CONTENTS

EXPLORING AUGMENTED REALITY

WEDNESDAY, NOVEMBER 16, 2016

U.S. SENATE,
COMMITTEE ON COMMERCE, SCIENCE, AND TRANSPORTATION,
Washington, DC.

The Committee met, pursuant to notice, at 3:06 p.m. in room SR–253, Russell Senate Office Building, Hon. John Thune, Chair- man of the Committee, presiding.

Present: Senators Thune [presiding], Wicker, Fischer, Gardner, Daines, Nelson, Klobuchar, Blumenthal, Booker, Manchin, and Pe- ters.

OPENING STATEMENT OF HON. JOHN THUNE,
U.S. SENATOR FROM SOUTH DAKOTA

The CHAIRMAN. Good afternoon. This hearing will come to order. I want to thank everyone for coming today to discuss the exciting potential of augmented reality technology.

This past Fourth of July weekend, many Americans began to no- tice an unusual phenomenon: more and more people—far more than usual—were going outside. Suddenly, sidewalks, parks, and local landmarks were packed with people wandering the great out- doors while burying their heads in their smartphones.

These people, of course, were playing the smash hit mobile game, Pokémon GO. But by going out into the real world to find and cap- ture digital creatures, they weren't just playing a game. They were getting their first exposure to the possibilities of augmented reality.

Many of us have heard of, or experienced, virtual reality, which usually involves putting on a headset that covers users' eyes, sur- rounding them in an artificial world. However, augmented reality, or AR, is different. AR takes digital information and superimposes it onto the real, physical environment. Rather than closing the user off from the real world, AR adds virtual content on top of the real world.

Pokémon GO accomplishes this by using a smartphone's camera to record the real world while the game displays digital characters over the image on the phone's screen. More advanced AR headsets, currently in development and in use by industry, have mixed re- ality capabilities that can map the user's surroundings in real time and allow virtual content to convincingly interact with the physical world.

These more advanced AR devices and techniques show that the potential of this technology goes far beyond smartphone games and could one day have a major impact on manufacturing, transpor- tation, medicine, and eventually the daily lives of average Americans. For example, imagine a worker in a factory whose job is to assemble an advanced jet engine for a new airliner. With an AR headset, that worker could see step-by-step instructions floating above his work station, with the exact spot he is supposed to weld being digitally highlighted.

Or imagine a medical student who can train on a virtual 3D model created from scans of a real patient. Or an EMT in a rural area who can receive real-time instructions from a specialist in a hospital hundreds of miles away on how best to stabilize a patient while help is on the way. AR technology promises to take all of the information that has been confined to the Internet over the past few decades and integrate it into the physical world, where such content can be most useful and do the most good.

Advanced manufacturing and other industries have already begun using AR for training new workers and have seen great improvements in safety and efficiency. We often hear about technology replacing workers, but AR provides an opportunity for technology to enhance workers instead, by helping them with their training and making them more productive.

In previous hearings this committee has held on new and emerging technologies, such as the Internet of Things and Autonomous Vehicles, I stressed how important it is for the government to avoid jumping in too soon with a heavy-handed regulatory approach. AR is no different. While there are certainly important policy questions to consider, such as the privacy of user data recorded by AR devices, it is essential that policymakers not unnecessarily stifle innovation. Instead, we should foster an environment that maximizes the potential benefits of this promising new technology.

There may be obstacles, regulatory or otherwise, to achieving the full potential of AR. Like a Pokémon trainer, the job of this committee is to "catch them all."

Earlier today, the Committee had the great opportunity to see AR in action firsthand. DAQRI, Niantic, and the U.S. Army Edgewood Chemical Biological Center provided us with a great demonstration of the Smart Helmet and a heads-up display for automobiles, which gives drivers important information without having to take their eyes off the road; Pokémon GO and other Niantic apps; and military-focused applications of AR.

Even though the only reality they could augment was the reality of the Russell Building, it was easy to see the potential of this new technology for a wide range of applications. I want to thank them for making their products available to us today.

I look forward to hearing from all of our witnesses to learn more about their experiences with AR and their visions for the future of this promising new technology.

I would say that we would recognize the Ranking Member, Senator Nelson, but I know he's on the floor, speaking, at the moment. So I think what we'll do when he arrives is give him an opportunity to make an opening statement, but proceed with the panel. I want to welcome all of our witnesses who are here today: Mr. Brian Blau is the Vice President of Research for Gartner, a technology research and advisory company. Mr. John Hanke is the Chief Executive Officer for Niantic, Incorporated, developer of Pokémon GO. Mr. Brian Mullins is the Co-Founder and Chief Executive Officer of DAQRI. Mr. Stanley Pierre-Louis is the General Counsel for the Entertainment Software Association, and Mr. Ryan Calo is an Assistant Professor of Law at the University of Washington.

I want to thank you all for being here and for taking the time to share the things that are going on in your world with us. As I said, we find it very exciting, and seeing firsthand some of the things that you all are doing here just a few minutes ago was— it's really cool. So we're delighted to have you all here. If you could confine your remarks to 5 minutes or thereabouts, and then we'll open it up to a few questions.

I'll start on my left and your right with Mr. Blau. So please proceed with your opening statement.

STATEMENT OF BRIAN BLAU, RESEARCH VICE PRESIDENT, GARTNER

Mr. BLAU. Chairman Thune, Ranking Member Nelson, and the members of the Committee, thanks for inviting me to testify about augmented reality. I'm Brian Blau, Research Vice President at Gartner, the world's leading information technology market research company. I'm here today because my background in immersive technology spans 25 years, including in my current position where I advise technology providers, CIOs, businesses, and investors across many industries and geographies on aspects of designing, marketing, and using personal devices, apps, and services. Let me begin by saying that if immersive technologies—and by that I mean augmented reality, virtual reality, and mixed reality— are to achieve their potential, several important issues need to be understood. First, using AR to blend the real world and virtual world in a seamless way can have novel and beneficial implications across a myriad of industries. This nascent technology is about to achieve a critical milestone: practical and affordable viewing devices entering the market. Now is our unique opportunity to foster its innovation and growth.

Second, the market for AR technologies might be small today, but interest, over the long term, remains high and the potential for growth is significant. Finally, for AR technologies to flourish, innovation needs to be supported and accelerated without undue restrictions. The result will be a plethora of new computing experiences that drive increased productivity across many industries; improved effectiveness of individuals in their work; and exciting new developments in the leisure, entertainment, and retail sectors.

The 50-year plus history of computing can't be told without including the technology that addresses how humans, using their senses, interact with computers, each other, and the world. With AR technology, users will perceive the physical world in new, richer ways, ones that are visually augmented to whatever best suits the needs of its users.

The technology brought before you today provides a prime example of American innovation, invention, and opportunity. Augmented reality, virtual reality, and mixed reality follow from a taxonomy of visual and sensory display types. AR devices are centered around a smart display, a transparent one, which can be worn on your head, maybe held in your hand, or even seen through a window.

Business use cases are broad. In coming years, field service workers, those that maintain utilities, infrastructure, machines, and equipment, will benefit because their work is often hands-busy tasks. An AR headset can provide visual overlays of diagrams, complex instructions, event recording, or enabling "see-what-I-see" remote collaboration. Using AR can improve workforce productivity by removing time-wasting behaviors or improving the efficiency of tasks.

The market for AR is mainly business today. We estimate the number of AR head-mounted displays sold in 2016 to be around several hundred thousand. We forecast that in 5 to 10 years, there will be hundreds of millions of head-mounted display devices in the hands of users, split between see-through transparent display devices and those that provide full immersion such as VR.

There are technology vendors competing for this opportunity—Microsoft, Google, ODG, Epson, DAQRI, and many others. First generation devices are available now. Next generations will exceed these capabilities, and improvements over the coming years will solve and optimize many perceptual computing challenges.

Not only will there be intense competition in hardware—the devices and the headsets—but there is also a great need for new core technologies as well as apps, services, infrastructure, and components, all of which need healthy digital ecosystems and business opportunities to flourish.

When will consumer AR become common? It may not be far off, and it's possible it will come in many form factors, including handsets and headsets. Use cases for consumer AR are quite compelling because the visual overlay technology can show real-time and instant information when we look out into the physical world.

Imagine turning your backyard into a video game, or going to a movie theater that is an individualized entertainment experience. For the market to grow, it's critical that you carefully consider any actions that would restrict or limit AR's innovation process. AR needs development and maturity in many areas and will for many years to come.

A particular focus should be around usability, safety, and security. The requirements are higher here. AR is the experience, and it could falter if the technology is restricted in ways that don't allow for experimentation, invention, testing, and ultimately broad use in many aspects of the consumer and business markets.

Thank you again for the opportunity to share our knowledge and guidance of this exciting application area and for the leaders of the U.S. Senate to take such a high level of interest.

[The prepared statement of Mr. Blau follows:]

PREPARED STATEMENT OF BRIAN BLAU, RESEARCH VICE PRESIDENT, GARTNER

Chairman Thune, Ranking Member Nelson, and the Members of the Committee:

Thank you for inviting me to testify today about augmented reality.

I'm Brian Blau, Research Vice President at Gartner, the world's leading information technology market research company. I'm here today because my background in immersive technology spans 25 years including in my current position where I advise technology providers, CIOs, businesses and investors across many industries and geographies on aspects of designing, marketing and using personal devices, apps and services.

Let me begin by saying, if immersive technologies, and by that I mean, augmented reality, virtual reality, and mixed reality are to achieve their potential, several important issues need to be understood.

First, using AR to blend the real world and virtual world in a seamless way can have novel and beneficial implications across a myriad of industries. This nascent technology is about to achieve a critical milestone—practical and affordable viewing devices entering the market. Now is our unique opportunity to foster its innovation and growth.

Second, the market for AR technologies might be small today but interest, over the long term, remains high and the potential for growth is significant.

Finally, for AR technology to flourish, innovation needs to be supported and accelerated without undue restrictions.

The result will be a plethora of new computing experiences that drive increased productivity across many industries, improved effectiveness of individuals in their work, and exciting new developments in the leisure, entertainment and retail sectors.

The 50-year plus history of computing can't be told without including the technology that addresses how humans, using their senses, interact with computers, each other and the world. With AR technology, users will perceive the physical world in new, richer ways, ones that are visually augmented to whatever best suits the needs of its users.

The technologies brought before you today provide a prime example of American invention, innovation and opportunity. Augmented reality, virtual reality and mixed reality, follow from a taxonomy of visual and sensory display types. AR devices are centered around a transparent smart display; which can be worn on your head, held in your hand, or seen through a wall.

Business use cases are broad. In coming years, field service workers, those that maintain utilities, infrastructure, machines, and equipment, will benefit because their work is often "hands-busy" tasks. An AR headset can provide visual overlays of diagrams, complex instructions, event recording, or enable "see-what-I-see" remote collaboration. Using AR can improve workforce productivity by removing time-wasting behaviors, or improving the efficiency of tasks.

The market for AR is mainly business today. We estimate the number of AR HMDs (head-mounted display headset) sold in 2016 to be around several hundred thousands. We forecast that in 5 to 10 years there will be hundreds of millions of HMD devices in the hands of users; split between see-through transparent display devices and those that provide full immersion such as VR. There are many technology vendors competing for this opportunity, Microsoft, Google, ODG, Epson, DAQRI and many others. First generation devices are available now. Next generations will exceed these capabilities, and improvements over the coming years will solve and optimize many perceptual computing challenges.

Not only will there be intense competition in hardware—the devices and headsets—but there is also a great need for new core technologies as well as apps, services, infrastructure, and components; all of which need healthy digital ecosystems and business opportunities to flourish.

When will consumer AR become common? It may not be far off, and it's possible it will come in many form factors including handsets and headsets. Use cases for consumer AR are quite compelling because the visual overlay technology can show realtime and instant information when we look out into the physical world. Imagine turning your backyard into a video game, or going to a movie theater that is an individualized entertainment experience.

For the market to grow it's critical that you carefully consider any actions that would restrict or limiting AR's innovation process. AR needs development and maturity in many areas and will for many years to come. A particular focus should be around usability, safety and security. The requirements are higher here; AR –is– the experience and it could falter if the technology is restricted in ways that don't allow for experimentation, invention, testing, and ultimately broad use in many aspects of the consumer and business markets.

Thank you again for the opportunity to share our knowledge and guidance on this exciting application of technology, and for the leadership of the U.S. Senate to take such a high level of interest.

Gartner

G00300520

Competitive Landscape: HMDs for Augmented Reality and Virtual Reality

Published: 21 October 2016

Analyst(s): Brian Blau, Annette Jump

Head-mounted displays and their use in AR and VR are quickly becoming a target of businesses due to their ability to enhance work and customer experiences. Ecosystem battles and years of fast device changes mean product managers should be selective and identify key verticals for immersive solutions.

Key Findings

- Ecosystem battles over the next five years mean that approximately five global players will dominate the market, but business verticals provide significant opportunities for value-added players.

- Diverse opportunity exists due to wide-ranging HMD capabilities. However, volume shipments will be small and less than 15 million units in the midterm and will ramp up to 35 million units by 2020.

- Devices are maturing quickly, but significant challenges remain. New product iterations are expected to be released constantly, so differentiation means specializing for a target audience.

- Selling to enterprise means educating IT about HMDs, the overall technical solution, support and services, and proof HMDs provide significant benefit to enhance the work process or improve customer scenarios.

Recommendations

For product managers:

- Aggressively build and market solutions, such as for field service, maintenance, training, design or medicine, which improve business functions using HMD technology.

- Become one of the top five ecosystem players, either globally, or in a specific use case, or in a vertical market segment, to gain and maintain market share.

- Work with ISV providers to enable a solutions channel to better help businesses integrate immersive technology enabling smart workplace environments.

- Create compelling user experiences for customers through great devices, but also help improve their technical expertise and design, and implement and continually refine solutions.

Table of Contents

8

Strategic Planning Assumptions

By 2020, 50% of the 50,000 largest businesses globally will have piloted or integrated immersive head-mounted displays (HMDs) for enterprise and customer use.

By 2020, there will be five HMD ecosystem providers that sell 80% of all devices.

By 2020, the market for HMD devices will exceed 35 million devices and generate $75 billion in revenue.

Analysis

The landscape for HMD for use in augmented reality (AR) and virtual reality (VR) solution spaces is quickly evolving, and the first ecosystems of devices, platforms and content are emerging in 2016. Gartner's definition of an HMD is a head-worn device that integrates small displays or projection technology. It is worn or mounted on or near the head so that its displays can be seen by the wearer at an ideal viewing distance, and aspects of the visual content will be contextual information that translates the wearer's state into visual cues.

The market for devices today is nascent but vibrant, and competition for the first deployment of devices into the market was well underway at mid-2016. Vendors are offering devices for augmented reality and virtual reality solutions, and these are typically defined as either having a transparent display (for AR) or one that is opaque (for VR). Form factors play heavily in how the devices are used and who would best benefit from them, and functionality greatly varies as devices are matched with software and services. Common form factors for VR include a facemask-style device that blocks the user's entire visual field of view, and AR devices can be found in glasses, helmets and clip-on form factors. Benefits range from entertainment experiences to enhancing the work process, but challenges in creating technology to integrate with the human perception of capabilities mean years of trial and development are needed before a high level of effectiveness is reached.

Gartner.

By mid-2016, the HMD vendor landscape was quickly gaining diversity. It spans from the largest technology providers, such as Google, Microsoft and Facebook, but also includes consumer electronics firms such as Samsung, Sony and Epson, and startups such as Atheer and Meta.

This report will reveal that while the market is new, it is already hypercompetitive and many of the biggest technology providers have announced or are planning on supplying or supporting HMD devices and ecosystems as part of their product portfolios. The unique nature of HMDs means many providers will use new and optimized OSes, and the associated hardware and software platforms, as well as enabling or supplying apps, services and content. Vendors that excel will be the ones that cover the entire HMD technology stack, as well as those that provide an ecosystem of solutions, that offer these devices and apps globally, or that partner to gain needed functionality.

This document will help product managers within HMD and other hardware providers to understand the evolution of HMD for different immersive solutions, the competitive landscape and major player positioning, as well as provide Gartner's view on the future of competition. This will enable them to decide on what parts of the HMD market they want to compete/enter, as well as better position and differentiate their products versus existing competition.

Competitive Situation and Trends

The Landscape for HMDs Coalesces in 2016

Outside of a few vendors, early access programs and smartphone VR (Google Cardboard or Samsung Gear VR), the sale of HMD devices to businesses and consumers started in 2016 to buyers that have been excited about their arrival. The devices, their content and apps greatly range in capability, price and performance, as vendors move quickly to provide solutions for a wide range of use cases.

By mid-2016, Gartner estimates that more than 7 million devices have made it into the hands of users, but overall usage has been limited to watching traditional flat-screen video, playing video games and businesses that are piloting HMD projects for future use cases. Business use of HMDs is less advanced than consumer use. This is due to fewer enterprise-ready devices being available compared with the consumer-ready VR headsets that are already in users' hands. The gap between the adoption of business use of HMD and consumer use will close, and by 2019 we will see HMD penetration rates where both segments of the market are well-established, and that business adoption could exceed consumer adoption.

Table 1 describes the main categories of devices and their market characteristics.

Gartner, Inc. | G00300520

Gartner.

Table 1. HMD Market Description in mid-2016

Form Factor	Description	Type	Target User	Examples
Fully immersive facemask style	**Smartphone VR** — an accessory; requires a smartphone for operation	VR	Consumer with mixed business use	Samsung Gear VR, Google Daydream and Cardboard
	All-in-One — self-contained; mobile/wireless	VR	Consumer and business	Intel Project Alloy, Sulon Q
	Wired/Tethered — connected to a PC with capable CPU/GPU or game console	VR	Consumer with mixed business use	Oculus Rift, HTC/Valve Vive, Sony PlayStation VR
Partially immersive with transparent display	Glasses, helmet, clip-on; all are mobile/wireless	AR	Business	Microsoft HoloLens, Daqri Smart Helmet, Vuzix M300

GPU = graphics processing unit

Source: Gartner (October 2016)

Overall, Gartner predicts that the market for HMD across all form factors — such as smart glasses, helmets, facemask style and others that enable AR and VR solutions — will see strong growth in a 10-year or more time frame, reaching $72 billion in device revenue in addition to apps and services. Through 2020, the market will see only modest growth, and acceleration of adoption will occur later once better consumer devices are made available. During this time period, we will see HMD adoption move from enthusiast levels to ones that show market maturity and global availability, and have sustaining business models. Based on Gartner's latest wearable forecasts, 477.8 million units of wearables devices will be shipped in 2020, which includes 39.9 million HMDs. More details around these forecasts can be found in "Forecast: Wearable Electronic Devices, Worldwide, 2016."

During our HMD forecast period through 2020, we expect technical functions of AR and VR to merge into a mixed reality feature set, and by then many midrange and premium HMDs will support a wide variety of immersive experiences. It is likely that the future HMD market linked with AR will be much bigger versus VR, mainly due to AR's horizontal applicability as a business tool. Additional factors, such as device and ecosystem maturity, cost of implementation, availability of vertical-specific solutions, and advancement of see-through display technology, will push forward a future type of immersion called "mixed reality." Superseding AR but still maintaining VR capabilities is this mixing of the real and virtual. This excites businesses and brands due to its ability to create hyperpersonal experiences. Getting to that mixed reality advanced point will require a mass market consumer see-through display solution, which we expect to see made available within five years.

Finally, by 2020, the number of market-share-leading HMD providers will diminish to approximately five, mainly due to the high technical requirements needed to make advanced transparent displays. The small group of two or three market share leaders will be the global companies that can create compelling consumer and business solution sets, namely ecosystems, where most of the list includes businesses that are already ubiquitous with consumers and business. In addition, we will see several providers that come from China, or that only focus on the market in Asia. There are opportunities to specialize in content and local technology ecosystems, such as ISPs or other digital content providers.

Supporting Different Ecosystems Is Key to Successful HMD Business Models

The successful HMD businesses will either be or support an ecosystem of devices, developer hardware and software platforms, operating systems, and content, similar to the Google Android and Apple iOS ecosystems we see today, or are ones that tightly integrate with them. That horizontal approach means flexibility in configuring HMD solutions, and controlling the technology and transaction flow, or being a platform for others to build on.

Other areas, such as providing content creation and management tools, professional services, infrastructure, components or being a geospecific provider in any of these areas, will be needed to support HMD providers or businesses that adopt HMD solutions. Figure 1 describes the layout of the HMD market for the next five years:

Figure 1. HMD Market Layout

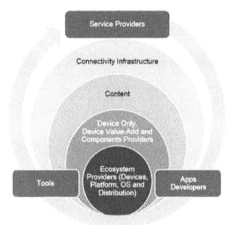

- **Ecosystem:** Market leaders
- **Devices Only:** Limited role
- **Devices Value-Add:** Nonglobal, niche, geospecific or other value that enhances the vendor offering
- **Components:** Support device providers and OEMs, displays, sensors/IoT and GPUs
- **Content:** Business process apps, immersive entertainment, games and 360-degree video
- **Service Providers:** Business partners needed due to lack of IT talent
- **Tools:** Workflow management, visualization engines, animation/3D and IT integration
- **Infrastructure:** Wireless and broadband communications transport

Source: Gartner (October 2016)

Business Models: Most HMD providers will focus on device sales directly to end users as their main business model, but we will see exceptions as provisions are made to allow businesses to purchase in volume. The largest HMD providers, those that will likely be the ecosystem leaders, will directly offer devices at no or low profit margins. An example is Oculus, which has previously stated it won't focus on profits for its device, but wants to enable its ecosystem and will provide the device at or near cost. Some HMD ecosystem leaders will provide OEM opportunities for others, such as the recently announced partnership between Intel and Microsoft (Intel Developer Forum [IDF] 2016), where each company will bring technology (Intel's Alloy HMD OEM specification) and Windows Holographic (Microsoft's OS for immersive devices). Ecosystem providers will also tax app developers for platform access, which is a typical type of revenue sharing we see in app stores such as those from iOS and Android.

Business Focus Is About Process Enablement and New Behavior Facilitation

We expect HMD technology to enable businesses to change how they manage individual work functions and to also empower employees in specific verticals. Businesses will use HMD technology to improve employee productivity, such as being used for training, in product design, when collaborating with others, in remote work situations, and other activities that can benefit from the use of head-worn displays.

In the short term to midterm, AR see-through display devices will be adopted by enterprises with consumer devices coming in several years at the earliest. A limited number of smart glasses and other HMDs for AR is available, but most are only for early adopters, and many HMDs have yet to ship their first commercially available units. We expect HMD product managers to select and focus on business verticals by offering their own cloud-based solutions, or that they will partner with third-party solution providers or independent software vendors (ISVs) to fill in product gaps.

For now, the focus for business-immersive HMD solutions is mostly on see-through AR devices targeted at basic work tasks, taking pictures, scanning codes or providing basic work process data. In mid-2016, there are many pilot projects underway for AR in logistics/warehousing, medical and healthcare, product design, business operations, retail, manufacturing, architecture, and more. If these pilots ultimately are successful, we will see greater adoption of HMDs in business verticals starting in 2017 and 2018.

Lack of IT HMD Talent Enables New Class of Professional Services to Help Integrate Immersive Technologies

Immersive AR and VR solutions require a different level of sophistication and enhanced user experience than other digital technologies to be effective. The success of HMD systems is heavily reliant on the experiences they enable, and IT's overall lack of engineering talent in 3D or graphics technology means services, not IT, will play an important experience design role for the next three to five years.

Some HMD systems, especially AR solutions for business, offer ecosystems and customization solutions — such as Atheer's AiR Suite — but few businesses are prepared from a technical or talent perspective to create and manage their own custom-made integrations and apps. Service providers in this sector, on the other hand, have that needed experience; for example, APX Labs, WorldViz and Eon Reality, each of which has been creating immersive content for businesses for more than 10 years. Service providers are adding to their knowledge arsenal with each new implementation, and as a result there is a growing cadre of providers that is becoming an important aspect of the market.

Where else can IT find examples of good HMD experiences and talent? The earliest consumer HMD adopters will be video game players who are avid buyers of the sophisticated graphics that make games attractive. These game developers are best prepared today to support AR and VR apps as they have the most experience working with graphical simulations and complex user experiences necessary for HMDs. Look to the consumer HMD experience for examples of best practices and expectations of better HMD apps and services.

The challenge for businesses and IT is threefold:

- They don't have the knowledge base to create effective solutions that can best leverage HMD devices

- They don't have IT staff that has experience in creating visualization or real-time graphics apps

- They are not familiar with example solution sets they can mimic and recreate for themselves

HMD product managers should focus on solving all three of these challenges by offering IT-friendly user interfaces, extended support and design consulting services, and advanced integrations with other IT systems to facilitate out-of-the-box data exchange. Until this advanced product feature stage is reached, build partnerships and solutions channels as there is a clear opportunity for solution providers to act as technical and design resources for IT.

Market Players

The following chart (broken into two parts as Figures 2 and 3) provides a high-level look at a cross section of the HMD provider landscape. Not all HMD solutions are listed, but ones representing all of the popular form factors are included. Some of the providers in this chart are further detailed in the Vendors to Watch section later in this document.

14

Figure 2. Sample Market Player Overview

Company	Picture	Portfolio	Release Status	OS	API	Example Vertical	Support	Region
Microsoft		HoloLens	Business/enterprise developers only	Windows 10	Yes	Manufacturing and operations, design, aerospace, automotive, space exploration, healthcare, education, retail	Through partners	U.S. and Canada
Google		Cardboard, Daydream View, Glass at Work	2014, October 2016, 2016	Android/iOS, Android, Glass OS	Yes	Cross-vertical support	None, For OEMs, Direct	Global, U.S., U.K., DE, CA, AU, U.S.
Oculus		Rift	March 2016	PC	Yes	Gaming and entertainment, retail	Direct, online community	U.S. and selected mature markets
Daqri		Daqri Smart Helmet	Developer edition	Daqri 4D OS	Yes	Manufacturing, oil and gas, transportation, utilities	Direct	U.S. and U.K./Ireland
Atheer		AiR Glasses	Prerelease, ships in 3Q16	AiR OS (Android based)	Yes	Field service, insurance, healthcare, oil and gas, warehousing/logistics	Direct	U.S.
Sony		PlayStation VR, SmartEyeGlass	October 2016, 2016	PlayStation, Android	Yes	Video games, business applications	Direct, Direct	U.S. and select mature markets
Epson		Moverio BT-200 and BT-300	BT-200 since 2014, BT-300 ships in 2016	Android	Yes	Business applications	Through partners	U.S. and select mature markets

DE = Germany, CA = Canada, AU = Australia

Source: Gartner (October 2016)

Figure 3. Sample Market Player Overview, Continued

Company	Picture	Portfolio	Release Status	OS	API	Example Vertical	Support	Region
ODG		R7	2016	ReticleOS, based on Android	Yes	Military and government, automotive, medical and entertainment, consumer (in future)	Directly and via partners	U.S. and select mature markets
Samsung		Gear VR	2014, last update in August 2016	Requires Samsung Android phone	Yes	Games and entertainment	Directly to users	Worldwide
HTC		Vive	2016	SteamOS	Yes	Games and entertainment	Online community	Worldwide
Meta		Meta 2	Prerelease	PC	Yes	Business applications	Direct, online community	U.S.
Vuzix		M100, M300	Available now, Select enterprise developers	Android, Android and iOS	Yes	Warehousing logistics, utility/field services, manufacturing, medicine, business apps, consumer (in 2017)	Directly and via partners	U.S., Europe and Japan
Baofeng		Mojing, in various configurations	2015	Android	Yes	Games and entertainment	Online community	China

Source: Gartner (October 2016)

Many other vendors have announced or offer HMD products, and it is thought that there are more than 100 vendors that have announced or are already shipping devices. Other vendors not listed above are Zeiss, Archos, LG, Razer, GameFace Labs, Fove, Recon Instruments (an Intel company), Optinvent, Kopin, Avegant, castAR, Canon, Innovega, Seebright, Lumus, Sulon, Avegant Glyph, Mattel, Vrvana, Brilliantservice, Scully and Starbreeze.

Magic Leap is included in this report due to its announced HMD and the large investment it received. More than $1.4 billion was invested in the company by 2Q16. There is a high level of interest surrounding Magic Leap in the technology community due to the large investment amount and patent filings that indicate an advanced level of HMD capability, but it has yet to demonstrate its devices so any claims of quality haven't been verified publicly.

The Future of Competition

One aspect of both AR and VR, and as mentioned several times, devices and systems will be advancing at a fast pace over the next five years. During this time, the basic functionality won't change, but the capabilities of HMDs will. One of the most profound changes will be the merging of device capabilities between AR and VR. Advances in transparent display technology as well as cameras and other sensors will be integrated into future HMD devices. The resulting data will provide more than enough data to allow developers to create both transparent and opaque apps on all types of devices. An important point for HMD product managers is to understand how AR and VR will merge functionality, and build that use case into future plans to allow for more flexible and useful systems.

HMDs Require Quality Experiences, or Risk Abandonment

Creating quality and effective immersive experiences aren't easy or intuitive, but can be achieved through an ongoing iterative design-test-release-improve process. HMD product managers need to enable a quality experience by providing robust ecosystems and platforms as well as devices that can fully enable these experiences. Without the combination of advanced device technology, the HMD market won't develop, and the likely cause will be due to user abandonment because of poor-quality experiences. Business demands for return on investment won't materialize if HMDs and their associated apps and services don't bring the benefits that are being advertised by providers today.

The Success of HMDs Relies on the Realization of Its Novel User Experience and Perceived Value

The hype around HMD technology has existed for decades, and vendors must deliver on the promises of an improved computing experience if users are trying and trusting that vendors can deliver on these promises.

It is unlikely that we will see a specific "killer app" for HMD linked with AR, as many implementations will be vertically targeted. In the midterm, we will see AR used around more advanced tasks in specific verticals (aerospace, medicine, universities, architecture/design and real estate), communication and collaborative work among mainstream business users and for remote work (oil/gas, repair workers in the field and car repairs/car accidents). Advanced capabilities, such as accurate overlays, simultaneous location and mapping (SLAM) or computer vision-assisted object identification, are available today for experimentation but won't be deployed in HMDs until a more advanced stage of development.

This change of the user interface, from flat to immersive, is a long-term challenge, and if the past is any indication of the future, it will take many years of advancement before these user interfaces will be refined to a point they can positively impact users at a reasonable cost. There is little real experience in the market for designing these immersive experiences, especially with IT, which seldom focuses on how its business users experience software systems.

Long-Term Value of HMD in Business Will Be Due to Democratization

Over the next two to three years, HMD quality will rise, out-of-the-box business systems will emerge, and prices of devices will decrease. This democratization of AR and VR will enable its adoption with affordability and functionality over time, then will match the ROI equation that businesses require.

Today, this means businesses will be identifying how they can integrate AR and VR solutions as a beneficial aspect of their workflow and process. They are accomplishing this goal by first working through pilot programs, which is how most HMD deployments start out. In future years, these pilots will become more robust and eventually lead to full-scale deployments, which will start in 2018 and 2019.

HMD product managers should facilitate pilot programs to help convince customers the value proposition of immersive use cases, such as by looking at ways to improve or change individual and physical workplace behaviors and actions into ones that can leverage HMDs. Solutions will likely need to be purpose-built for a single task, but this can be accomplished with standardized devices and systems. Most businesses will not need purpose-built or ultra-expensive VR, but will be able to create prototype and deployable VR solutions for less than $100,000 by 2018.

Hurdles Remain Before Devices and Their Systems Become Robust

The HMD available today is usable. While advanced in nature, it is considered an entry-level product compared with what will be available in just a few years. There are many areas of development needed before HMD devices can better match a human perceptual system, or provide core business value. Figure 3 lists many areas of development and research that are ongoing at device vendors and content developers.

Figure 4. HMD Technical and Business Challenges

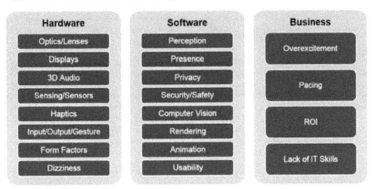

Source: Gartner (October 2016)

One area of particular concern is the ability of the HMD to best match the human perceptual system. One physical reaction to HMD use is dizziness or headaches, and users simply won't continue wearing an HMD if these conditions persist. Solving this problem requires better technology, including improving the display, optics or even adding eye-tracking. Ultimately, though, it is the combination of device and app that drives each experience, and when done correctly most people won't have a negative response, such as being dizzy.

Issues such as human factors and perception are long-term concerns for HMD providers, and as much as they can create great technology, product managers must work with content providers in unison to create the best devices possible. As AR and VR are complex solutions, not individual technology pieces, each must work well together to overcome these challenges as we have yet to see any one single device or system component be dominant.

Competitive Profiles

Microsoft

Market Overview

Microsoft is a relatively new player in the HMD market with its HoloLens product. It announced the prototype HoloLens in January 2015, and the Development Edition was launched in March 2016. Microsoft HoloLens is a fully self-contained holographic computer that is able to deliver an AR experience, which Microsoft calls "mixed reality." It is also the only HMD device that is running on Windows 10. Windows Holographic OS was recently updated with AR-specific versions of Microsoft

Outlook Mail and Calendar, allowing users to interact with emails and calendar appointments in a virtual world. For now, Microsoft's focus with HoloLens is only on the business segment, but inclusion of video game demos indicates its focus may include consumers in the next two to three years.

How This Provider Competes

A mobile and wireless head-mounted display, Microsoft HoloLens is available to developers in the U.S. and Canada, with some broader availability across selected mature markets expected in 2017. The device has an optical system that integrates a variety of sensors to capture information about user actions and the surrounding environment. It also understands gestures and is able to generate multidimensional full-color images using a special transparent display. The device has more processing power than the average notebook and its holographic processing unit (HPU) is able to process the large volume of data required to deliver a smooth virtual experience. This enables users to move freely and naturally interact with virtual data and content.

The biggest current limitation of Microsoft HoloLens is around its field of view, which is limited to approximately 30 degrees. The company is now proactively building its developer community to create apps for a wide variety of business verticals. Microsoft's strategy is to provide best-of-class immersive technology, and to work with partners to enable a growing ecosystem of devices, apps and services, which gives Microsoft some advantages in the HMD market due to its existing influence in business.

Google

Market Overview

Google offers three classes of HMD devices: Cardboard, Daydream and Glass at Work.

Cardboard was launched in 2014 as a technical commentary piece indicating that VR didn't need to be complicated or expensive. The idea caught on, and today there are dozens of smartphone-based VR systems that use the Cardboard app standard. By mid-2016, Cardboard-style devices dominate the HMD market by unit volume, and while it is not a significant revenue generator for Google, the devices are accessible to many, including a special version that is made available to elementary school teachers.

Google's latest push into VR is Daydream, first announced in May 2016 with follow-up details in October 2016. Daydream is a VR platform that includes a smartphone VR HMD, a handheld controller for VR user interactions, an operating system tailored to support VR experiences, a developer platform and content distribution. Google's new Pixel smartphone is the first marketed as Daydream-ready, and device specifications let OEMs offer their own HMD devices, the first of which are expected in late 2016. Partners that are expected to release devices include Samsung, HTC, Huawei, LG, ZTE, Asus, Alcatel, Xiaomi and others. Google's YouTube, Play Movies, Photos and Street View — plus games and apps such as Netflix and Hulu — will be part of the initial content at the device launch in October 2016.

Glass Explorer Edition prototypes had an initial limited release beginning in April 2013, followed by a public release in May 2014. The project received a mixed reaction from both consumers and enterprises. The intense media coverage generated by this initiative uniformly raised awareness for HMDs, as well as AR and VR. Glass operates through a wireless connection to a smartphone. Google's Glass at Work is an update to the original device and is available to select developers that focus only on enterprise solutions. Its small screen, limited battery life and lack of a true AR experience, as well as public backlash over privacy concerns, ultimately limited the appeal of Glass.

How This Provider Competes

Google's overall approach to HMDs is focused on being a global ecosystem of devices, content, OSes and developer tools. In addition, Google has invested significant funds into Magic Leap, which could mean that Google will have access to yet more HMD technology in the future. Google's other efforts, such as overall development of Android, and Project Tango's computer-vision-driven sensor technology, will influence and enhance their HMD efforts. Their approach is broad and extensive, and represents the most diverse strategy and offering of any other player in the market.

Oculus/Facebook

Market Overview

Oculus was acquired by Facebook in April 2014, and since then the company has invested heavily in its technology and talent. The much-anticipated HMD Oculus Rift was released in March 2016. The device's $599 price is lower than others, but it also requires a PC to operate, significantly raising the cost of an entire Rift system to approximately $1,500, and it is supported only in Windows PCs. Oculus Touch, an ergonomic gesture controller, will sell for $200, and additional cameras for room-scale VR raise the cost of an overall system.

Additionally, Facebook has been working with Samsung on a smartphone VR, the Samsung Gear VR, which is powered by immersive software from Oculus. Samsung Gear VR has been available since late 2014, and while the unit price is $99, it is often given away free with a new Samsung smartphone purchase. Oculus powers Gear VR software, and in October 2016 it announced that more than 400 apps and games are available.

How This Provider Competes

While the Oculus Rift is available for sale to any type of user, its focus is concentrated on consumers, gaming and entertainment. Facebook's recently announced studio works to enable VR games and content production for its HMD. It has also created the Oculus Store, which offers Rift-compatible games and content. All of its games come with an "intensity" rating based on how much motion there is in the game to help users judge the possible impact of VR, especially for novice players. There is also a growing list of movies and apps that are supported for the VR experience on the Oculus Rift.

Gartner

Oculus is being challenged by competition from traditional technology providers such as Microsoft and Google. Outside of Samsung, Facebook has no hardware partners that could challenge it, as developers will want to limit the number of systems they support as the market continues to expand. Oculus announced in October 2016 that it will spend another $250 million to support content and app developers to help seed the market.

Daqri

Market Overview

The main HMD product of Daqri, a U.S. company, is the Daqri Smart Helmet, which enables workers via AR experiences to get more information about their environment. In the form factor of a safety helmet, the device is meant for on-site workers and offers build-in optimized work instructions and other hands-busy tasks. The HMD runs Daqri 4D OS, and the company also offers software to help businesses integrate the helmet functionality into their workflows.

How This Provider Competes

The Smart Helmet device is for enterprise users. The targeted verticals are manufacturing, oil and gas, transportation and utilities. The idea is to use AR to deliver specific work instructions and reduce errors in quality, and reduce unnecessary movement of employees in factories and production facilities, as well as increase efficiency through data visualization. Customers are able to use Daqri 4D Studio to create custom work packages and then use them with the Smart Helmet. It is possible to integrate data from ERP systems with both 4D Studio and its HMD device. The company is also offering Melon, an activity monitor for your brain (electroencephalography [EEG] monitoring) that can help users to track and train focus and related behaviors.

The Daqri Smart Helmet is currently available only to approved businesses, and Daqri's formal developer program opens in November 2016. With few selected customers and partners on board, there is no commercial availability yet.

Atheer

Market Overview

Atheer created its first prototype of 3D AR glasses in 2013, and has been shipping Atheer AiR Glasses since December 2014. The focus of the company is making users of selected verticals more productive through an AR-like interface. The currently available product is AiR Glasses, mobile 3D AR glasses with touch-free gesture control. The device uses an Android variant, which means it is compatible with a large number of apps. It also has a medium-wide field view (50 degrees) and offers eight-hour battery life, which gives it an advantage over others that can't yet provide these same capabilities.

How This Provider Competes

Atheer aims to empower workers to interact with the digital world similarly to how they do it in the real world. Atheer AiR Glasses allow users to visualize and interact with data via gestures, and do it touch-free and precisely. Atheer is able to provide immersive and wide-field computing, as well as personalized binocular image optimization. The company is focused on enterprise with the following vertical focus: field service, insurance, healthcare, oil and gas, and warehousing/logistics. The company also offers an enterprise-ready cloud solution — the Atheer AiR Suite platform. It provides collaboration, task-flow management and remote expert communication.

Its software suite is able to support the company's own-branded smart glasses, as well as those from other providers, such as Epson, Osterhout Design Group (ODG), Recon and Vuzix. This unique approach means flexibility in providing devices themselves, or supporting those from other vendors.

Market Overview

Initially announced at GDC 2014, Sony's PlayStation VR will connect to the PlayStation 4 (and Pro) and provide VR games and entertainment content. Sony's device is based on a helmet and straps to the head so that the fully immersive display rests on the forehead and is counterbalanced with a weight on the back, versus being strapped from the rear as seen in other VR HMD solutions. Sony has a long-standing history with game players through the PlayStation platform, and these players are Sony's intended audience at launch. Devices became available in October 2016.

Sony's SmartEyeglass devices are AR-style smart glasses and run on the Android operating system. SmartEyeglass uses a prism to bend the image around the headpiece, but it is small enough to fit comfortably into a glasses-like package.

How This Provider Competes

Sony's approach to HMDs is concentrated on its PlayStation game console and consumers. The PlayStation is the leading game console with more than 40 million devices in the hands of consumers, which is far ahead of its main competitor, Microsoft Xbox, which is not yet offering any HMD or VR solutions. Due to the large installed base, it is expected that the PlayStation VR will become the market leader by unit volume in the months after the device makes it to the hands of game players.

Sony's HMD SmartEyeglass device competes with the others that are targeting business users, which is an increasingly crowded market.

Gartner

Epson

Market Overview

The company started developments around HMD (smart glasses, specifically) in 2009 and introduced its first product, Moverio BT-100, in 2011. Since then, the company has expanded its offering to smart glasses (Moverio BT-200/BT-300) and a smart headset (Moverio Pro BT-2000). Epson's BT-2000 headsets cost $2,999 and are targeted at industrial verticals. Epson's BT-200 smart glasses have been in the market from 2014 and cost $699. Its price is much less expensive versus newer models, 20% heavier versus newer models, has only a video graphics array (VGA) camera, and won't fit over regular glasses, which are some of the differences. The next-version BT-300 is claimed to be the lightest smart glass device in the market, and has been announced for preorders, but no pricing or availability date has been released.

How This Provider Competes

Epson's product portfolio of HMDs is targeted specifically at enterprise users. Its smart glasses allow users via a transparent display to seamlessly blend digital content into the physical world around them. A front-facing camera enables AR, while via head-tracking sensors users can have a 360-degree digital canvas. Epson's smart headset is specifically designed for industrial working environments (logistics, construction, remote workers and airspace), so it features an adjustable headband, allows motion tracking with 3D mapping and gesture control, and is dust and water resistant. All of Epson's HMDs are built on the Android OS, which provides a familiar OS development platform for many app developers.

Osterhout Design Group (ODG)

Market Overview

The HMDs from ODG are AR devices fashioned in the form of electronic glasses. Its latest product is R-7 smart glasses, priced at $2,750. The R-7 model incorporates sensors typically found in most AR glasses devices, such as gyroscopes, magnetometers and accelerometers, have a voice recognition system, a front-facing camera and global navigation satellite technology. They include stereoscopic see-through displays in which the user sees graphics overlays or other contextual information. This way, the user is able to maintain awareness of the surroundings. In January 2016, ODG reached an agreement with 21st Century Fox to acquire a minority stake in the company. The main benefit for ODG will be the access to huge media content and apps through its integration of the Android operating system.

How This Provider Competes

ODG's background as an HMD supplier to the U.S. Department of Defense has given it years of experience creating immersive devices for a very focused customer. The company's smart glasses are targeted at verticals such as automotive, medical and entertainment, as well as its traditional customers in the military and government. For now, the company is only playing in the business segment and plans to expand into the consumer market in the future.

Samsung

Market Overview

Samsung's partnership with Oculus has resulted in the Gear VR, a smartphone-based HMD that relies on a specific set of Samsung Galaxy smartphones, such as the Note 7, for its functionality. Software powering the Gear VR is from its partner Oculus, which provides the VR user interface, app store and developer platform. The Samsung Gear VR is the global leader of this type of HMD, but Chinese Baofeng has more devices in the hands of users and it can use many types of smartphones for its operation.

How This Provider Competes

Samsung's strategy with the Gear VR is more than just its HMD, as it is the top provider of smartphone devices worldwide. Samsung now offers a suite of devices that support its overall VR efforts. The Gear 360 is a spherical camera that takes pictures and video that can be seen in VR experiences. Also a partner of Google's Daydream, it is expected that its next generation of devices will include phones that support Google's new VR headset.

Vuzix

Market Overview

Vuzix has HMDs available for purchase by enterprises or consumers. Its long history in the HMD market (since 1999) gives it experience in creating devices, as well as brand recognition in the market. For the enterprise space, the company offers several smart glasses (the M100, which is available now, and the M300, which is available to select enterprise developers). The currently available M100 smart glasses cost approximately $983. In January 2015, the company received a $25 million investment to accelerate the development of fashion-oriented smart glasses for the consumer space. Currently, Vuzix offers iWear Video, which is a wearable display for gaming, mobile video and VR. The approximate cost of iWear Video is $590.

How This Provider Competes

The vendor's catalog of HMD devices comprises two categories: AR glasses for enterprises and iWear for a wearable display. The M100 is different from other smart glasses in that it supports a single screen (monocular), and the unit can attach to any pair of consumer prescription glasses or conforming safety glasses. The display is not transparent, but a front-mounted camera adds some realism to the imagery.

iWear is a VR device in a visor-like form factor. It can play back movies or be used as an HMD for VR experiences, similar to Oculus. Vuzix M100 smart glasses are running Android OS, so they are compatible with many of the existing Android apps. The next generation of Vuzix smart glasses (M300) will be able to operate on both Android and iOS.

Gartner.

The company also announced plans to release in Fall 2016, M3000 smart glasses with advance waveguide optics. The upcoming Vuzix device will have features and capabilities similar to a smartphone, but in a hand-free wearable form factor.

References and Methodology

This report was prepared using primary and secondary resources extensively. The research uses additional industry sources to verify the accuracy of the information. Sources of data used by Gartner include, but are not limited to, interviews with HMD and solution providers, media reports and general trade press, published HMD provider statements and documents, estimates from reliable industry sources, and the Gartner analyst community.

Various companies, government agencies and trade associations may use slightly different definitions of product categories and regional groupings, or they may include different companies in their summaries. These differences should be kept in mind when making comparisons between information provided by Gartner and information provided by other research organizations.

Gartner Recommended Reading

Some documents may not be available as part of your current Gartner subscription.

"Forecast: Internet of Things — Endpoints and Associated Services, Worldwide, 2015"

"Forecast: Wearable Electronic Devices, Worldwide, 2016"

"Top 10 IoT Technologies for 2017 and 2018"

"Hype Cycle for Personal Technologies, 2016"

"Enabling Future Smart Workplaces With IT"

"Predicts 2016: Know Your Customer to Capture Opportunities in the Personal Technologies Market"

This document is published in the following Market Insights:

Computing Hardware Worldwide
Consumer Services Worldwide
Mobile Communications Worldwide
Mobile Devices Worldwide

Gartner: AR/VR HMD Devices Market Forecast

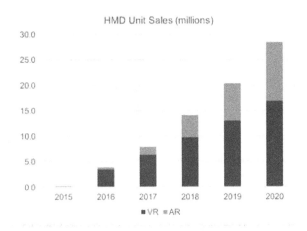

HMD Unit Sales (millions)

- Availability of devices starts in 2016
- Quality HMD's for VR, AR lacks maturity
- Adoption accelerates at modest pace through 2020
- Not a large market, consumer AR not yet a factor

Source: Forecast Wearable Electronic Devices Worldwide 2016

Gartner.

Gartner: AR/VR HMD Revenue Forecast

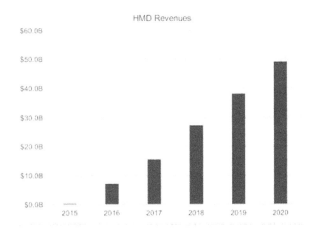

HMD Revenues

- US: design and develop
- Asia/China: components and assembly
- Display technology for AR isn't robust. Sensor data fusion lacks scale
- Critical R&D investment period
- Apps/services revenues to exceed HMD revenues as much as 2x-5x

Source: Forecast Wearable Electronic Devices Worldwide 2016

Gartner.

Gartner Hype Cycle 2016: Example AR Technologies

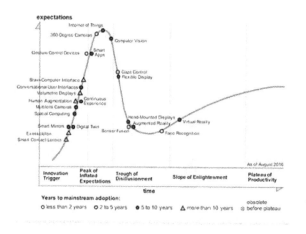

- This chart shows sample technologies from Gartner Hype Cycle 2016 related to AR, VR, and head-mounted displays
- AR/VR: older inventions, quickly maturing
- New technologies classes:
  - Augment human performance
  - Measure deep biometrics
  - New digital experiences

Source: Gartner Hype Cycle 2016

Gartner

The CHAIRMAN. Thank you, Mr. Blau.

And I apologize for mispronouncing Mr. Calo's name.

Mr. Calo, please proceed.

That's what I get for not wearing my glasses.

Mr. CALO. No worries.

STATEMENT OF RYAN CALO, LANE POWELL AND D. WAYNE GITTINGER ASSISTANT PROFESSOR, UNIVERSITY OF WASHINGTON SCHOOL OF LAW, AND FACULTY CO-DIRECTOR, UNIVERSITY OF WASHINGTON TECH POLICY LAB

Mr. CALO. Chairman Thune, Ranking Member Nelson, and members of the Committee, thank you very much for this opportunity to discuss the promise and the perils of augmented reality.

Augmented reality, of course, has many positive applications, from training tomorrow's workforce to empowering people with disabilities. But the technology also raises novel concerns that companies and policymakers must address if augmented reality is to be widely adopted and positively affect American society.

The University of Washington Tech Policy Lab, which I co-direct, is a unique interdisciplinary research unit at the University of Washington that aims to help policymakers develop wise and inclusive technology policy. We have studied augmented reality and its impact on diverse populations and discuss our findings in detail in a white paper entitled *Augmented Reality: A Technology and Policy Primer,* which we made available to the Committee.

Our research suggests that augmented reality raises a variety of questions of law and policy, including around free speech, privacy, and potentially novel forms of discrimination and distraction. So just to give a couple of examples, will the constant recording of one's environment give hackers, companies, and government unparalleled access to the bedroom, the boardroom, and private spaces? Could the superimposition of information over reality render AR users, in some instances, vulnerable or unsafe? And are there situations, like job interviews, where knowing everything about an individual in real time could result in discrimination or subject the AR user to legal liability?

So having studied this area, we developed essentially five recommendations that are very broad in nature, and I wanted to go over them in my remaining time, if I may.

The first is that we should recognize that augmented reality is actually advancing quite rapidly, right? And so law and policy, in order to stay relevant, should not assume a fixed instantiation of augmented reality over time. I mean, I can point to many examples where we've passed measures that assumed technology would stay a certain way, but it changed and those measures became outdated.

The second is to conduct threat modeling. Threat modeling is a computer science idea that has to do with anticipating what adversaries will do with these systems. So we think that a careful and thorough model of seeking who might want to compromise AR systems without preconceptions—such as no one would ever do that—is crucial. And it's especially crucial in instances like these, where a compromised system could actually cause physical harm to users.

We think it's important to coordinate with designers. Ultimately, technologists need to be aware of the values that society holds and that policymakers hold, and policymakers, in turn, need an accurate mental model of the technology in order to make wise decisions. So this hearing, for example, is a great example of the dialog between the designers and the manufacturers and policymakers.

We think it's extremely important to consult with diverse stakeholders. People will experience AR quite differently, depending on their characteristics, their experiences, and their capabilities. So take children, for example. Children will experience augmented reality quite differently. People who are incarcerated and so forth will experience it quite differently. It creates opportunities and dangers, depending on the individual.

And then, finally, we expect that policymakers and designers will acknowledge the potential tradeoffs. For example, the long-term information storage in cloud processing and other advanced data processes may ultimately result in faster performance or more complex functionality, but then potentially at a cost of privacy. So perfection can be the enemy of the good. But, ultimately, it's crucial to understand that the architectural decisions that are made, the design decisions, have these kinds of policy implications.

With that, thank you again for the opportunity to testify, and I'm happy to hear your questions.

[The prepared statement of Mr. Calo follows:]

PREPARED STATEMENT OF RYAN CALO, LANE POWELL AND D. WAYNE GITTINGER ASSISTANT PROFESSOR UNIVERSITY OF WASHINGTON SCHOOL OF LAW, AND FACULTY CO-DIRECTOR, UNIVERSITY OF WASHINGTON TECH POLICY LAB

Chairman Thune, Ranking Member Nelson, and Members of the Committee, thank you for the opportunity to discuss the promise and perils of augmented reality.

Augmented reality (AR) refers to a mobile or embedded technology that senses, processes, and outputs data in real time, recognizes and tracks real-world objects, and provides contextual information by supplementing—or in some cases, replacing—human senses. AR differs from so-called virtual reality in that AR users continue to experience most of their physical environment. AR has many positive applications, from training tomorrow's workforce, to empowering people with disabilities.

But the technology also raises novel or acute policy concerns that companies and policymakers must address if AR is to be widely adopted and positively affect American society.

The UW Tech Policy Lab is a unique, interdisciplinary research unit at the University of Washington that aims to help policymakers develop wise and inclusive technology policy. We have studied AR and its impact on diverse populations and discuss our findings in detail in the appended white paper *Augmented Reality: A Technology and Policy Primer.*

Our research suggests that AR raises a variety of question of law and policy, including around privacy, free speech, and novel forms of distraction and discrimination. For example: Will the constant recording of a user's environment give hackers, companies, and government unparalleled access to the bedroom, the boardroom, and other private spaces? Could the superimposition of information over reality render the AR user vulnerable or unsafe? And are there situations—such as job interviews—where knowing everything about an individual could result in discrimination or subject the AR user to legal liability? Industry must design AR products with these and many other questions in mind.

Thank you again for the interest in our research and the opportunity to appear before the Committee. I look forward to your questions.

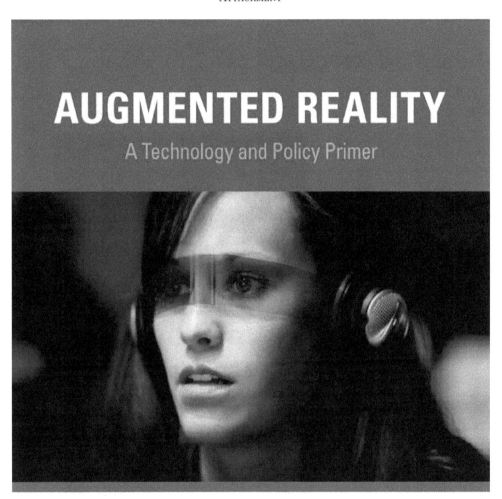

AUGMENTED REALITY

A Technology and Policy Primer

TECH POLICY LAB

AUGMENTED REALITY: A TECHNOLOGY AND POLICY PRIMER

Tech Policy Lab, University of Washington, September 2015

Visitors to the Haunted Mansion ride at Disneyland may recall the moment when, passing by a long mirror, ghostly figures appeared riding alongside them in the cart. This effect was an early and fun example of augmented reality (AR), a set of technologies that overlay information onto everyday experience.

The vision for AR dates back at least until the 1960s with the work of Ivan Sutherland. In a way, AR represents a natural evolution of information communication technology. Our phones, cars, and other devices are increasingly reactive to the world around us. But AR also represents a serious departure from the way people have perceived data for most of human history: a Neolithic cave painting or book operates like a laptop insofar as each presents information to the user in a way that is external to her and separate from her present reality. By contrast, AR begins to collapse millennia of distinction between display and environment.

Disneyland park's encounter a "ghost" in the Haunted Mansion.
Image source: www.disney.com

Today, a number of companies are investing heavily in AR and beginning to deploy consumer-facing devices and applications. These systems have the potential to deliver enormous value, including to populations with limited physical or other resources. Applications include hands-free instruction and training, language translation, obstacle avoidance, advertising, gaming, museum tours, and much more.

Using the Word Lens app to translate a menu in real-time. Image source: www.blogcdn.com

A traveler app displaying information about the New Orleans area. Image source: www.wikipedia.org

Heads-up display overlaying to provide turn directions and features overview. Image source: www.pinimg.com

AR also presents novel or acute challenges for technologists and policymakers, including *privacy, distraction, and discrimination.*

This whitepaper—which grows out of research conducted across three units through the University of Washington's interdisciplinary Tech Policy Lab—is aimed at identifying some of the major legal and policy issues AR may present as a novel technology, and outlines some conditional recommendations to help address those issues. Our key findings include:

1. AR exists in a variety of configurations, but in general, AR is a mobile or embedded technology that senses, processes, and outputs data in real-time, recognizes and tracks real-world objects, and provides contextual information by supplementing or replacing human senses.

2. AR systems will raise legal and policy issues in roughly two categories: collection and display. Issues tend to include privacy, free speech, and intellectual property as well as novel forms of distraction and discrimination.

3. We recommend that policymakers—broadly defined—engage in diverse stakeholder analysis, threat modeling, and risk assessment processes. We recommend that they pay particular attention to: a) the fact that adversaries succeed when systems fail to anticipate behaviors, and that, b) not all stakeholders experience AR the same way.

4. Architectural/design decisions—such as whether AR systems are open or closed, whether data is ephemeral or stored, where data is processed, and so on—will each have policy consequences that vary by stakeholder.

The whitepaper follows a method developed by our Lab for examining new technologies. The method, which also provides a roadmap for the whitepaper, consists of the following elements:

We work with technologists—in this case, computer science professors and students—to define the technology we are examining as precisely as possible.

We look to the humanities and social sciences—here, information science—to think through the impact of the technology on various stakeholders. Mindful that non-mainstream voices are seldom represented in tech policy discussions, we have developed a formal process of refining our analysis with diversity panels, i.e., panels of individuals whose experience or expertise lies outside of the tech mainstream.

We engage with law and policy researchers to uncover assumptions jurists and policymakers might hold that no longer make sense in light of the new technology.

We offer a set of conditional recommendations that depend upon the particular values and goals policymakers, broadly construed, are trying to achieve.

ONE: TOWARD A WORKING DEFINITION OF AR

Augmented reality is shaping up to be an important and widespread technology. Some specific examples of AR being marketed or developed today include: Google Glass, Microsoft's HoloLens, Sony's Smart EyeGlass, Meta's Space Glasses, Magic Leap, Navdy Automotive, Across Air, and Word Lens.

Google Glass product image from Google Glass creative sheet; right image from https://www.youtube.com/watch?v=9c6W4CCU9M4

As these examples show, there is no easy definition of "augmented reality"; AR is best understood as a class or family of technologies that tend to have certain common and distinguishing features. We have identified six such features, most of which are present in most AR systems:

1. *Sense properties about the real world.* The system will collect various forms of data about the world as the user experiences it. Sensors may include video (e.g., depth cameras, cameras worn on the body), audio, haptic input (i.e., detecting physical touch), location (e.g., GPS, GSM triangulation), motion, or wireless signals (e.g., WiFi, Bluetooth).

2. *Process in real time.* Inputs from the sensors will be analyzed and used by the system in real time. Some information may be stored for later analysis or sharing (e.g., life-logging), but at least some of the data is used in real time.

3. *Output (overlay) information to the user.* Information gathered and processed by the system will generally be overlaid on the user's usual perception of the world; this is unlike virtual reality, which entirely replaces the user's setting with a new environment. In augmented reality, information may be conveyed to the user via a variety of devices, including a screen, a speaker, or haptic feedback (e.g., vibrations, air pulses). Researchers are even experimenting with visual feedback via contact lenses.

4. *Provide contextual information.* The information provided by the system to the user is contextual and timely, meaning it will relate to what the user is currently experiencing. For example: real-time in situ language translation, ratings for restaurants passed on the street, or arrival time updates while waiting at the bus stop.

5. *Recognize and track real-world objects*. The feedback will tend to track or process real-world objects or people in the user's view. For example, a facial recognition application may recognize faces and label them with names as the identified person moves through the user's field of view.

6. *Be mobile or wearable*. In the long term, we expect that many augmented reality systems will be wearable (e.g., AR glasses), and the majority of our analysis will focus on such systems. However, a system does not need to be wearable to technically be considered an AR system; mobile options include some smartphone applications and heads-up displays in cars. Similarly, the Xbox Kinect facilitates many AR applications, but is not itself mobile.

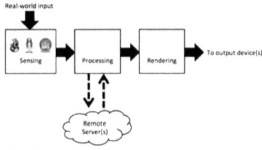

This definition helps distinguish AR from previous and constituent technologies while encompassing a burgeoning variety of AR applications. AR is still a young technology, so design choices are evolving and have yet to become industry standards. These choices in turn will drive the capabilities of AR, its impact on people, and its ramifications for law and policy.

One design parameter that warrants special attention is the *operating system* (OS), i.e., the underlying software platform or firmware that dictates the system's basic architecture. Full fledged AR will run on an OS—Google Glass, for instance, runs on a modified version of the Android OS and Microsoft's HoloLens will run on Windows 10.

The configuration of the OS drives other choices: whether to open the platform to applications (apps) or other third party innovation; whether and how long to store information; whether to process information locally on the device or on a remote server; and whether the information is processed by a computer system, by a person (through crowdsourcing), or some combination. We also note that data collected from an AR system can be combined with other data sets, and brought together in the processing and display.

Further design decisions relate to the *interface*, how the user perceives and interacts with the system. Such issues include: whether and how to notify the user—and others—that an AR system is actively recording; the user's control over various parameters such as the access the system gets to her social media, email, or other accounts; and what information she perceives. Each of these choices affects not only the performance and versatility of the system but the ways AR interacts with the contemporary legal system.

TWO: HOW AR AFFECTS HUMAN EXPERIENCE

BMW Augmented Reality changing guides in the absorber strut position.
Image source: BMW Augmented Reality www.bmw.com/en/topics/fascination-bmw/augmented-reality.html

AR systems change how people can interact with each other and their environment. AR users perceive more (or less) than the person, place, or object actually before them, as information is overlaid on their view of the world. They can also record their surroundings for future analysis. AR can confer new information in real time or alter the user's actual experience or skillset: someone who is poor at remembering faces can receive a prompt reminding him of where he met the person he is talking to, while someone without technical knowledge of cars could be guided through how to change a fan belt.

AR also changes the experiences of the people around the user, whose features and actions may now be recorded and analyzed—with or without notice, depending on designer choices. Moreover, AR makes it possible that two or more people perceive the same environment differently. One person may perceive an environment in an augmented state, while another may not. Two people may both experience an augmented space, but their versions may consist of different information overlays.

Not everyone experiences AR the same way, i.e., as "augmenting" reality by introducing new sensory information. For some populations—notably, those living with disabilities—AR may fully or partially replace a sense. Thus, for instance, an assistive technology may vibrate as people or objects approach or convert auditory information to visual stimuli. Those living with disability may come to rely upon these signals, such that their sudden interruption could create an inconvenient or even dangerous sensory deficit. These and other non-mainstream experiences must be kept firmly in mind when enumerating the potential use cases of AR, and as we contemplate rules and possible exceptions.

AR systems may also prove both empowering and disabling for a given population depending on the context. For example, AR could empower incarcerated youth providing a wider range of educational experiences, including hands-on work that would otherwise require intense investment in physical tools or spaces. But AR could also hinder these populations to the extent their arrest or incarceration records are rendered more visible to friends and neighbors, landlords, law enforcement, or prospective employers. Similarly, though AR could reveal, distract, and imperil people in new ways, it could also empower them by permitting them to record their surroundings, communicate with others, and gain information while keeping alert and not looking down.

THREE: CHALLENGES FOR LAW AND POLICY

AR systems change human experience and, consequently, stand to challenge certain assumptions of law and policy. The issues AR systems raise may be divided into roughly two categories. The first is collection, referring to the capacity of AR devices to record, or at least register, the people and places around the user. Collection raises obvious issues of privacy but also less obvious issues of free speech and accountability. The second rough category is display, referring to the capacity of AR to overlay information over people and places in something like real-time. Display raises a variety of complex issues ranging from possible tort liability should the introduction or withdrawal of information lead to injury, to issues surrounding employment discrimination or racial profiling. Policymakers and stakeholders interested in AR should consider what these issues mean for them.

Issues related to the collection of information include:

1. *Reasonable expectations of privacy.* Constitutional, tort, and much statutory privacy law (such as wiretap restrictions) turn on whether an action violates a citizen or consumer expectation of privacy that society is prepared to accept as reasonable. The introduction of always-on recording devices into public and private spaces may cause societal expectations to shift in ways that further diminish privacy recourse. Or, alternatively, such devices may place so much pressure on the reasonable expectation doctrine that courts may choose to revisit its utility.

2. *The third party doctrine.* U.S. case law holds that citizens have a diminished expectation of privacy in information (e.g., bank records) that they willingly convey to a third party (e.g., the bank). AR systems have the potential to relay virtually all the activity of a user to third-party servers for storage and processing. As with the reasonable expectation of privacy test generally, this development will make government access to the daily lives of citizens easier or call the already scrutinized third party doctrine into further question.

3. *Free speech.* The First Amendment right to free speech is a well-known right backed by a highly developed body of case law; more and more courts are beginning to recognize a corollary right to record and gather information as a prerequisite to expression or as expressive conduct in itself. The right tends to be a function of two factors: where the recorder is, and who (or what) is the subject of the recording. The routine use of AR may, again, strain this burgeoning doctrine. There is also an attendant concern that government will take countermeasures and seek to block the use of AR, limiting its potential as a tool of accountability.

4. *Intellectual property.* The always-on recording of everyday life will inevitably capture work that is protected by copyright, trademark, or other intellectual property laws. This risk may be particularly acute in movie theatres, concerts, or business settings. The mere collection and analysis of protected work is unlikely to trigger liability for most AR functions – for example, an application that displays the name of the song the AR user is hearing. Yet we can imagine a diverse array of situations in which copyrighted work is broadcast or superimposed, or in which trade secrets are compromised. The fair use doctrine may be frequently implicated in some of these scenarios, but since fair use is considered a defense to claims of infringement – rather than an exemption – its applicability will always be tested only after the fact, complicating the decision-making of technologists and policy makers concerned with how to regulate AR use and functionality in real life contexts.

Issues related to display of information include:

1. *Negligence.* AR systems overlay information onto the world in real-time. If users rely on this information in error, or if the information distracts a user, then any resulting injury could lead to a cause of action for negligence. Imagine, for instance, a heads-up display in the windshield of a vehicle that places an advertisement over a stop sign. The defendant could be the user herself, the manufacture of the AR system, an individual app developer, or all three.

2. *Product liability.* As a general matter, information, ideas, or expressions do not qualify as "products" for the purpose of product liability. Thus, for instance, the publisher of a book about edible mushrooms is not liable to readers who eat poisonous mushrooms in reliance on the book. But AR systems do more than relay information; they blend information with everyday activities in ways that can blur the distinction between real and perceived environments and risk physical harm. This could lead to a new category of product liability at the intersection of information and object.

3. *Digital assault.* AR can make objects appear that are not there, and disappear objects that are. Accordingly, there is the prospect of purposively harming or instilling fear in an AR user. This photo shows a prank involving the superimposition of a spider onto someone's hand—a mild example, but AR advertisers and others may decide to employ shocking visuals and other effects to get attention. Under current theories of American tort law, purposively placing someone in imminent apprehension of physical harm—even where no harm is possible—can constitute a tort.

4. *Discrimination.* AR will make it possible for users to look up information about people and places in real-time. The information gained in this fashion could lead to adverse decisions that are normatively unfortunate and even illegal. Anti-discrimination laws prevent decision makers from factoring some pieces of information into their decisions—for example, in employment, housing, or a number of other contexts. Imagine a jurisdiction that does not allow employers to consider an applicant's arrest record or marital status while making hiring decisions. An AR system that provided an applicant's rap sheet or dating profile automatically would be problematic under this regime. In other cases, though a form of discrimination may not specifically be proscribed, it is often best to remain ignorant of such information to limit liability exposure. More broadly, the display of crime statistics, housing prices, or other information about a building or neighborhood could further isolate urban and other environments by conveying an often false sense of danger.

FOUR: (CONDITIONAL) RECOMMENDATIONS

This whitepaper defines AR, provides a basic technical description, envisions implications for human experience, and identifies some of the unique or acute legal and policy issues raised by the possibilities of AR. This final section discusses options available to various policymakers who have an interest in promoting or regulating the technology. We identify a set of best practices and explain the interaction between various technical decisions and the law and policy landscape. The recommendations are "conditional" in the sense that they do not purport to advance any particular vision, but rather provide guidance that can be used to inform the policymaking process, regardless of the specific values any individual policymaker—or group of policymakers—may seek to advance.

1. *Build dynamic systems.* AR technology is advancing rapidly. Today's systems should be flexible and capable of updating in the face of technical and cultural change. Law and policy itself, to stay relevant, should not assume a fixed instantiation of AR for all time.

2. *Conduct threat modeling.* Adversaries succeed in defeating systems precisely by finding behaviors that designers didn't anticipate. A careful and thorough model of who might seek to compromise AR systems and how—without preconceptions ("no one would ever do that")—is critical to managing privacy and security risks. Threat modeling is especially crucial where, as with AR, a system compromise could cause physical harm.

3. *Coordinate with designers.* Neither the design of AR nor the design of technology policy should occur in isolation. Technologists may not be aware of certain values held by policymakers and may not appreciate the legal import of a particular design decision. Policymakers, in turn, need an accurate mental model of the technology in order to make wise decisions—including omitting to take action.

4. *Consult with diverse stakeholders.* People will experience AR very differently, depending on their characteristics, experiences, and capabilities. Academia and industry interested in widely useful AR should expressly consult with diverse populations and solicit and incorporate their feedback.

5. *Acknowledge tradeoffs.* Design decisions matter. A system that is open to third party analysis or contribution—from open source code to an app store—may promote greater freedom and innovation, even as it opens consumers up to potentially malicious applications. Long-term information storage, cloud processing, and other advanced data processes may result in faster performance or more complex functionality, but at potential costs to privacy and free speech. Perfection can be the enemy of the good, but identifying important values and describing how architecture affects them is critical to responsible innovation in and beyond AR.

CONTRIBUTORS

The following people from the Tech Policy Lab contributed to this whitepaper:

Ryan Calo, JD

Tamara Denning, PhD (computer science)

Batya Friedman, PhD (information science)

Tadayoshi Kohno, PhD (computer science)

Lassana Magassa, PhD candidate (information science)

Emily McReynolds, JD, LLM

Bryce Clayton Newell, JD, PhD (information science)

Franziska Roesner, PhD (computer science)

Jesse Woo, JD

Thank you to the participants in our Diversity Panels, whose insights contributed greatly to this whitepaper.

Cover Image Credit: Leonard Low, via Wikimedia Commons, http://bit.ly/1b6Xtu

To learn more about the Lab, visit us at techpolicylab.uw.edu.

BIBLIOGRAPHY

Books, Articles, & Papers

Babaguchi, N., Koshimizu, T., Umata, I., & Toriyama, T., *Psychological study for designing privacy-protected video surveillance system: PriSurv,* In: "Protecting Privacy in Video Surveillance" at 147 (Springer-Verlag 2009).

Brassil, J., *Technical challenges in location-aware video surveillance privacy,* In: "Protecting Privacy in Video Surveillance" at 91 (Springer-Verlag 2009).

Butler, D. J., Huang, J., Roesner, F., & Cakmak, M., *The privacy-utility tradeoff for remotely teleoperated robots,* In: Proceedings of the 10th Annual ACM/IEEE International Conference on Human-Robot Interaction (2015).

D'Antoni, L., Dunn, A., Jana, S., Kohno, T., Livshits, B., Molnar, D., Moshchuk, A., Ofek, E., Roesner, F., Saponas, S., Veanes, M., & Wang, H. J., *Operating system support for augmented reality applications,* In: Proceedings of the USENIX Workshop on Hot Topics in Operating Systems. (2013).

Deng, J., Krause, J., and Fei-Fei, L., *Fine-grained crowdsourcing for fine-grained recognition,* In: Proceedings of the IEEE Conference on Computer Vision and Pattern Recognition (2013).

Denning, T., Dehlawi, Z., & Kohno, T., *In situ with bystanders of augmented reality glasses: Perspectives on recording and privacy-mediating technologies,* In: Proceedings of the 32nd Annual ACM Conference on Human Factors in Computing Systems (2014).

Felt, A. P., Ha, E., Egelman, S., Haney, A., Chin, E., & Wagner, D., *Android permissions: User attention, comprehension, and behavior*, In: Proceedings of the Symposium on Usable Privacy and Security (2012).

Friedman, B., Kahn Jr, P.H., & Borning, A., *Value Sensitive Design and information systems*, In: "Human-computer interaction in management information systems: Foundations" at 348 (Armonk 2006).

Friedman, B., Smith, I. E., Kahn Jr, P.H., Consolvo, S., & Selawski, J., *Development of a privacy addendum for open source licenses: Value Sensitive Design in industry*, In: Proceedings of the ACM International Joint Conference on Pervasive and Ubiquitous Computing (2006).

Gupta, S., Morris, D., Patel S.N., Tan, D., *Airwave: non-contact haptic feedback using air vortex rings*, In: Proceedings of the ACM International Joint Conference on Pervasive and Ubiquitous Computing (2013).

Halderman, J. A., Waters, B., & Felten, E. W., *Privacy Management for Portable Recording Devices*, In: Proceedings of the Workshop on Privacy in Electronic Society (2004).

Hayes, G. R., & Truong, K. N., *Selective Archiving: A Model for Privacy Sensitive Capture and Access Technologies*, In: "Protecting Privacy in Video Surveillance" at 165 (Springer-Verlag 2009).

Hoyle, R., Templeman, R., Armes, S., Anthony, D., Crandall, D., & Kapadia, A., *Privacy behaviors of lifeloggers using wearable cameras*, In: Proceedings of the ACM International Joint Conference on Pervasive and Ubiquitous Computing (2014).

Jana, S., Molnar, D., Moshchuk, A., Dunn, A., Livshits, B., Want, H. J., and Ofek, E., *Enabling fine-grained permissions for augmented reality applications with recognizers*, In: Proceedings of the USENIX Security Symposium (2013).

Jana, S., Narayanan, A., & Shmatikov, V., *A Scanner Darkly: Protecting user privacy from perceptual applications*, In: Proceedings of the IEEE Symposium on Security and Privacy (2013).

Jung, J., & Philipose, M., *Courteous Glass*, In: Proceedings of the Workshop on Usable Privacy & Security for Wearable and Domestic Ubiquitous Devices (2014).

Kooper, R., & MacIntyre, B., *Browsing the Real-World Wide Web: Maintaining Awareness of Virtual Information in an AR Information Space*, 16 International Journal of Human-Computer Interaction 425 (2003).

Mark Hornyack, P., Han, S., Jung, J., Schechter, S., and Wetherall, D., *"These aren't the droids you're looking for": Retrofitting Android to protect data from imperious applications*, In: Proceedings of the 18th ACM Conference on Computer and Communications Security (2011).

McPherson, R., Jana, S., & Shmatikov, V., *No Escape From Reality: Security and Privacy of Augmented Reality Browsers*, In: Proceedings of the 24th International World Wide Web Conference (2015).

Ng-Thow-Hing, V., Bark, K., Beckwith, L., Tran, C., Bhandari, R., & Sridhar, S., *User-centered perspectives for automotive augmented reality*, In: Proceedings of the IEEE International Symposium on on Mixed and Augmented Reality (2013).

Paruchuri, J. K., Cheung, S. C. S., & Hail, M. W., *Video data hiding for managing privacy information in surveillance systems*, EURASIP Journal on Information Security (2009).

Patel, S. N., Summet, J. W., & Truong, K. N., *BlindSpot: Creating capture-resistant spaces*, In: "Protecting Privacy in Video Surveillance" at 185 (Springer-Verlag 2009).

Raval, N., Srivastava, A., Lebeck, K., Cox, L. P., & Machanavajjhala, A., *MarkIt: Privacy Markers for Protecting Visual Secrets*, In: Proceedings of the Workshop on Usable Privacy & Security for Wearable and Domestic Ubiquitous Devices (2014).

Roesner, F., Denning, T., Newell, B.C., Kohno, ,T., Calo, R., *Augmented Reality: Hard Problems of Law and Policy*, In: Proceedings of the ACM International Joint Conference on Pervasive and Ubiquitous Computing (2014).

Roesner, F., Molnar, D., Moshchuk, A., Kohno, T., & Wang, H. J. *World-Driven Access Control for Continuous Sensing Applications*, In: Proceedings of the ACM Conference on Computer and Communications Security (2014).

Schiff, J., Meingast, M., Mulligan, D. K., Sastry, S., & Goldberg, K., *Respectful Cameras: Detecting Visual Markers in Real-Time to Address Privacy Concerns*, In: "Protecting Privacy in Video Surveillance" at 65 (Springer-Verlag 2009).

Sutherland, I. E., *A head-mounted three-dimensional display*, In: Proceedings of the Fall Joint Computer Conference, American Federation of Information Processing Societies (1968).

Templeman, R., Korayem, M., Crandall, D., & Kapadia, A., *PlaceAvoider: Steering first-person cameras away from sensitive spaces*, In: Proceedings of the 21st Annual Network and Distributed System Security Symposium (2014).

Vilk, J., Molnar, D., Ofek, E., Rossbach, C., Livshits, B., Moshchuk, A., Wang, H. J., & Gal, R., *SurroundWeb: Mitigating Privacy Concerns in a 3D Web Browser*, In: Proceedings of the IEEE Symposium on Security and Privacy (2015).

Cases

Chicago Lock Co. v. Fanberg, 676 F.2d 400 (9th Cir. 1982)

Glik v. Cunniffe, 655 F.3d 78 (1st Cir. 2011)

Katz v. US, 389 U.S. 347 (1967)

Smith v. Maryland, 442 U.S. 735 (1979)

United States v. Jones, 132 S.Ct. 945 (2012)

Winter v. G.P. Putnam's Sons, 938 F.3d 1033 (9th Cir. 1991)

The CHAIRMAN. Thank you, Mr. Calo.
Mr. Hanke?

STATEMENT OF JOHN HANKE, FOUNDER AND CHIEF
EXECUTIVE OFFICER, NIANTIC, INC.

Mr. HANKE. Mr. Chairman, Ranking Member Nelson, and members of the Committee, my name is John Hanke. I'm the Founder and Chief Executive Officer of Niantic, Inc., a mobile gaming company headquartered in San Francisco, California. On behalf of the 75 dedicated and innovative professionals at Niantic, it is an honor to be here before you today to talk about augmented reality, or AR, something we're very excited about.

We launched Pokémon GO this last summer, and I want to talk about that in more detail. But before we discuss Pokémon GO, I want to just talk a little bit about the things that led up to the development and launch of that product.

Prior to that, I spent about 7 years at Google heading up our maps and geo-location efforts. So this included the development and launch of products like Google Earth, Google Maps, Street View, and so on. During that time period, the iPhone was created and launched, Android was created and launched, and we began to think about ways to use that geo-location and mapping technology for new kinds of products. At the same time, we were anticipating the development of augmented reality hardware. We see it as an evolution from the cell phones that exist today to wearable computing to the kinds of glasses and devices that you saw demonstrated earlier today.

Our philosophy is to go out and build products for the billions of cell phones that exist today and then to gradually adopt these new forms of augmented reality hardware as they enter the marketplace. We conceived of a group to go out and pursue that opportunity called Niantic, and we really had three goals for that group. The first goal was to create applications using this new mobile geo-location AR tech to get people outside and moving around. This was a very personal thing for me, as a father of three, at the time my eldest son was still at home. He just left for college. But he was spending a lot of time playing *Minecraft*. I love *Minecraft*. It's an amazing application. But, you know, we live in California. It's nice outside. There are lots of interesting places to go, and I wanted to create an app that would have the same kind of draw for him in terms of those compelling qualities but to be used outside, and it would be something that kids and parents could do outside. So we had this goal of encouraging kids and people to go outside.

The second goal was exploration and discovery of information about the places that we live. I'm kind of a history buff, and so we had this idea that if we could surface historical information about your community or places that you visit that it would help people build a connection with the town that they live in. It would be informative for kids and would just generally be a good thing. So that kind of exploration was the second kind of key tenet of our group.

The third was about encouraging real social interaction between people. So we hear a lot about social today, but it's usually in the context of social media, which means sending a message or a photo to somebody online. With mobile technology, we see a huge opportunity to build applications that actually encourage people to go outside together and have fun in groups and have face-to-face real human social interaction. So encouraging that type of behavior was the third major goal for the group.

We launched a couple of applications before Pokémon GO, an app called "Field Trip," which I showed some of you earlier today, which focuses on historical information. We launched a game called "Ingress," which has now been downloaded 20 million times around the world. It's kind of our cult hit. And then this last summer, we launched Pokémon GO.

So we are 75 people. We worked really hard on that product. We felt like it would be successful. But I have to say that we were pretty overwhelmed and shocked by the reception that it met during this last summer. It was an incredible 2 months for us of just watching that unfold, and it was incredibly gratifying to see people enjoying the product that we built, to see people out in parks in California and New York, Michigan, Florida, everywhere in between, and parents and kids playing together. We heard all kinds of positive stories from people about how the app helped get them outside and helped them have fun together with their friends.

It was an intense amount of work for us to keep that product up and running, just to add the number of servers that we needed to keep the product functioning, and to deal with the fact that, in this day and age, even though we're a 75-person startup, we had an international product to deal with, which means that we had to deal with interfacing not only with policymakers here in Washington and city governments and mayors across the United States, but with your equivalents in countries around the world.

So for a small startup company, that's pretty overwhelming. You know, we're trying to understand policy. We're trying to understand how to communicate with people literally in dozens of countries around the world. So we've been working through that over the course of the past two months.

I think because of the kind of frenzy around Pokémon GO, there are a lot of issues that came up that are related to policy, and I'm happy to have a chance to discuss some of those with you today. There are some things that I think we do really well that I want to talk about, some misunderstandings, and some challenges.

In terms of things that we do really well, COPPA and COPPA compliance is something that I think we are best in industry. We went out with a fully COPPA compliant login process. That means if you are 13 or under, you have to get parental consent to create an account to play the game, and we worked with our partners at the Pokémon Company in order to create that, and we're very proud of that work. As I mentioned, many of us in Niantic are parents, and protecting our children is very important to us.

A misconception has to do with data, and you heard it mentioned earlier today. There are people who look at augmented reality and assume that vast amounts of data are being vacuumed up and stored. It's been our policy to collect only the minimum amount of data that is necessary to operate our game.

So whenever you see Pokémon GO—and we demonstrated it earlier today—there's a camera view. You can see the background. You see the Pokémon hopping around. There are some people that have said, "Oh, we're collecting all that imagery data," so if there's a person in the background or something in the background, that's all being retrieved and stored on Niantic servers. That's not the case. None of that stuff is transmitted to us.

People have said that we're collecting vast amounts of personally identifiable information or to sell that to advertisers. That's not the case. Our business is about an app purchase. It's a very successful business model for us. It does not incentivize us to try to collect the kinds of personal identifiable information that other people are trying to collect. So we collect the minimum amount that we need to operate the game, and we do not sell that or provide that to third parties.

An area where we've met some challenges is in the area of what I would generally classify as hacking, and that word means a lot of things to different people. But we've had many individuals and groups around the world try to access our servers, to try to steal our intellectual property, to basically try to build applications that inappropriately pull data from our servers, allow people to cheat in the application, and do things that are harmful to our business, and we often feel like we're out there alone in trying to fend off these attacks.

It is kind of a Wild West situation. It doesn't always feel like there's a sheriff out there to help out, and it's a big challenge for us. It consumes a lot of our resources, and for small startups out there that are trying to launch applications into this environment, it's a very difficult challenge, and it's an area where, frankly, I think more help would be welcome.

So we're very excited about AR. I think it's the next major transition in technology from the cell phone to AR. That means it is not a billion dollar opportunity. It is a hundreds of billions of dollars opportunity. It's a great opportunity for American companies and for startups.

So thank you again, Mr. Chairman and Senator Nelson. I'm happy to be here to talk to you and to answer your questions.

[The prepared statement of Mr. Hanke follows:]

PREPARED STATEMENT OF JOHN HANKE, FOUNDER AND CHIEF EXECUTIVE OFFICER, NIANTIC, INC.

Introduction

Mr. Chairman, Ranking Member Nelson, and members of the Committee, my name is John Hanke, and I am the founder and Chief Executive Officer of Niantic, Inc., a mobile gaming company headquartered in San Francisco, California. On behalf of the 75 dedicated and innovative professionals at Niantic, it is an honor to be here before you today to talk about augmented reality, or "AR," and specifically, the current state of AR technology, where it's going, and what lessons we have learned that would be of interest to you as policymakers.

We understand today's hearing may in part be due to the extraordinary global response to Niantic's latest mobile app, Pokémon GO. We are particularly proud that this game has helped to turn the world's attention to the current reality and enormous potential of AR for entertainment, education, and community-building.

With that said, I know I speak for all of my colleagues at Niantic when I say that what we experienced following the game's launch in July far exceeded our own imaginations. As we rolled out the game, the immediate reception was almost surreal. My wife e-mailed to tell me that Jimmy Fallon and Stephen Colbert are talking about Pokémon GO. Professional athletes and celebrities began tweeting pictures from the app of themselves with Pokémon. Thousands signed up for a Pokémon walk on the National Mall here in Washington, and a similar walk in San

Francisco. How this game insinuated itself into everyday conversation and pop culture in and outside the United States sparked even greater interest and usage.

Since July, the app has been downloaded over 600 million times, and is enjoyed by users in more than 100 countries. And it's just been a little more than four months.

With the unanticipated popularity of the game, we had a couple of outages as we scaled up, and of course, hacking was a constant and costly nuisance. With help from our former colleagues at Google, we quickly arranged for server expansions to keep up with demand. We also made critical adjustments to deal with hacking.

Since early October, things have settled into a more manageable pace. After the initial sprint, our team was exhausted, but elated. It's been rewarding for all of us to see people young and old enjoy something that we worked so hard to create. We've heard and continue to hear stories about people getting outside, spending time with their friends and family, meeting new people and discovering new places in their communities. These stories speak directly to our core mission with augmented reality—to use technology to get people off their couches and outside to appreciate the wonder of the world around us.

Augmented Reality and Niantic: The Hidden Story of How We Got Here

Niantic is focused on using existing mobile technology to augment what we see outside before our very eyes. It's important to clarify what we mean when we talk about AR. The term "augmented reality" was first coined by a researcher at Boeing in 1990 to describe a system that overlaid graphics onto a display of physical reality. The primary early adopters of this technology in the 1990s were in military and medicine. By 2002, an article in *Popular Science* called augmented reality the "killer app in portable computing," but back then, to recreate what you can now see today through your smartphone required twenty-six pounds of off-the-shelf equipment strapped to your back.

It's often said here in Washington that public policy struggles to keep pace with innovation, but when I imagine someone in 2002 walking with a heavy backpack of first generation augmented reality gear, it reminds me of a simple truth we have in Silicon Valley: Innovation struggles to keep up with our own imagination.

As I look at my own experiences with technology, I've sought to bring innovation a little closer to my own imagination. There are a number of critical developments in telecommunications and information technology, from improved processing power to wireless broadband, that helped bring augmented reality to everyday consumers, but two critical factors for me in particular were maps and games.

As I was growing up in Cross Plains, a small town in central Texas, I'd read National Geographic and pull the maps out. So it's no surprise that I would later combine my fascination with programming with my love of maps. In 2000, I was part of a team that started a company called Keyhole, which was later acquired by Google and became the foundation for Google Earth. At Google, I also led the team that launched Google Maps, and other "Geo" products and services.

It was great to be at Google and channel my map and travel-inspired imagination from my boyhood to the innovations I was creating as an adult. And it led to the creation of "Field Trip," the first smartphone app we created at Niantic. Field Trip uses Global Positioning System technology and a database of information about places to deliver cards containing interesting information about a user's immediate surroundings as she walks through the world. The app automatically surfaces these bits of educational and historical information, including local history, interesting landmarks, and works of art and architecture as a user moves through the world. If we were walking by the Transamerica Building in San Francisco, for example, and passed a historical marker affixed to the building, Field Trip would show a card with the origin of our company name: the whaling ship, *Niantic*. This ship brought fortune-seekers to Yerba Buena—later renamed San Francisco—during the California Gold Rush in 1849. Run aground in the harbor and abandoned by its crew, the *Niantic* was converted into a storeship and hotel that would repeatedly catch fire and be rebuilt. Today's San Francisco Financial District is where the *Niantic* first ran aground, and remnants of the ship were excavated at the foot of the Transamerica Building in 1978. The *Niantic* serves as a wonderful metaphor for the types of hidden stories surfaced through our products: The knowledge exists—it just may not be always available to us.

In addition to maps, I've always enjoyed games, and like so many of my generation, writing code for games on cassette tapes that could be read by a TRS–80 eight-bit computer was a wonderful introduction to computer programming. And even before I started Keyhole, I worked on several of the first commercially available, Internet-based massively multiplayer online games.

So it seems both logical and linear that my dual passions for mapping and multi-player gaming would result in Niantic's second mobile app and first augmented reality game, Ingress. With Ingress, by building a game on top of the map data from Google Maps, we could combine gaming, walking, and exploring. An added motivation for me in developing Ingress and the Niantic platform was to help solve a common modern parenting issue with screen time. My oldest son, twelve at the time, shares my love of games. I knew that games got me into programming and I didn't want to take that away from him, but I also wanted him to get out from in front of a game console and see the world around him.

We launched Ingress in November 2012, and today, the Ingress community is amazing, and continues to grow as we approach our four-year anniversary, with more than one million active players in 4,000 communities worldwide. In fact, when Pokémon GO launched in the United States, I was in Japan for an Ingress event, and it was our largest event ever, with more than 10,000 users.

The Lure, Lore, and Logistics of Pokémon GO

The popularity of Ingress among the gaming community, particularly in Japan, gave rise to the notion of combining the long-cherished Pokémon franchise with maps and AR technology.

If you think about the lore of Pokémon, you can understand why it worked well in an AR context. As depicted in the animated series, the player (called a "Trainer") goes out into the world searching for and capturing Pokémon. Through your device—your phone today and perhaps some kind of glasses or other devices in the future—you become the Trainer and can see this fantastical world of Pokémon overlaid on the real world. Pokémon GO is exactly what's depicted in the story of Pokémon, and a great example of bringing our innovations a little closer to our imaginations.

Much has been written and discussed about the PokéStops and Gyms you see in Pokémon GO, and it's worth sharing briefly how we decided their locations, which go back to the origins of Niantic Labs and the evolution and development of our earlier products. Many of the historical markers and other local landmarks from our first app, Field Trip, became significant game locations ("portals") in Ingress. While further developing Ingress, we thought about how to expand this set of interesting places that are public, visually recognizable, and appropriate places for people to visit. We asked Ingress players to submit their ideas for local landmarks they thought would be great additions to the game; millions of places were suggested, and a subset of those submissions (such as the Children's Museum in Brookings, South Dakota and the Kennedy Space Center Visitor Complex in Florida) was added to the existing set of points of interest to populate Pokéstops and Gyms in Pokémon GO.

Lessons Learned Along the Way

As with any new technology, the use of AR for gaming applications like Ingress and Pokémon GO has sparked many questions that have public policy implications here in the United States and globally. I look forward to answering your questions shortly, but let me highlight a few key areas:

Children's Online Privacy: Teen and adult players are the primary intended player base for Pokémon GO, but we recognize that the game will be of interest to some children under the age of 13 who have access to a smartphone. For this reason, we created a verifiable parental consent mechanism to comply with the Children's Online Privacy Protection Act ("COPPA"). Consistent with the requirements of COPPA, potential new users are asked to enter their birthdate in an age screen prior to signing up for the game. Potential players who enter a birthdate under age 13 are directed to the Pokémon Trainer Club, operated by The Pokémon Company International, and their parent is provided an e-mail notice that they are interested in getting access to play Pokémon GO. A parent of an under-13 can work through the steps of the Pokémon Trainer Club to (1) create an online account; (2) provide certain forms of information to verify their identity; and (3) accept our Terms of Service and Privacy Policy.

The Pokémon Company International collects certain information from parents (such as name, date of birth, and certain information, such as a Social Security number) to obtain verified consent as required by COPPA. It does not share this information with Niantic. Additionally, parents have the option to provide certain personal information, such as their child's name, to The Pokémon Company International as part of the account sign up process; Niantic does not obtain this information.

A parent can always notify us to exercise their right to refuse collection, use, and/or disclosure of their child's personal information. And if we learn that an under-13 account was created without parental consent, that account and all other personal information collected in conjunction with that account will be deleted.

Data Integrity: Let me say up front that Niantic does not and has no plans to sell Pokémon GO user data—aggregated, de-identified or otherwise—to any third party.

Pokémon GO does collect and store certain information that interacts with various settings on the user's mobile device to provide core game functionality and improve Niantic's services. For example, the app collects and stores certain location information in order to show the Trainer on the map, and to trigger the resources, such as Pokémon, Pokéstops and Gyms that appear in her area. If a Trainer chooses to play with "AR" mode turned on, the app accesses the camera viewer in order to display the Pokémon "in real life" as you may have seen during the demonstration prior to the hearing. As you would expect, this information about the user's performance and activity is stored in connection with a user's account. The app also collects certain information to improve our services, and to facilitate important quality and stability objectives. For example, Niantic collects network provider information to allow for better quality geo-location.

The app collects information when it is open; there is no background collection of data in normal play mode. When the application is open, it disables the mobile device setting that automatically puts the phone to sleep when there has been no interaction by the user for a certain period of time. This is a key feature needed for Pokémon collection activities while a Trainer is moving around. When the user puts the phone to sleep manually, however (such as through pressing the power button), Pokémon GO goes idle.[1]

User Safety and Intellectual Property: As I noted earlier, since the app was launched, Pokémon GO has been a target of numerous hacking efforts, including distributed denial of service attacks, unlawful data collection from our services, and monetization through the use of botnets and other devices. We are concerned about these apps and services because in many cases they put our users at risk, and also because of the misuse of our intellectual property.

For example, a backdoored version of the game was found on a file repository service not long after the game was launched. Attackers also sought to lure potential Pokémon users to malicious sites that mimicked our own site, claiming users would be given additional features if they referred friends to the site, which led to more spamming. We've also seen strains of malware masquerading as Pokémon GO-related apps.

In these cases, as in others, working internally and with our licensors and partners, we've been able to take certain malicious apps and sites down, but these challenges raise important questions about what technical and legal resources we have to combat efforts to misuse if not malign our intellectual property. It certainly underscores the need for review of existing laws to allow innovators to protect their intellectual property and systems from unauthorized use, particularly where the safety and security of users is at stake.

Conclusion: Where Will Augmented Reality Take Us?

Mr. Chairman, the most often asked question I now get can be expressed in two words: What's next? For us at Niantic, we're working on new sets of features for both Ingress and Pokémon GO, and planning for future titles. We enjoyed releasing some fun elements of gameplay for Pokémon GO tied to the Halloween weekend, and we look forward to additional releases to further enhance the game experience.

For the broader industry, tech leaders ranging from Apple's Tim Cook to Microsoft's Satya Nadella share my view that the potential of augmented reality far surpasses virtual reality. Indeed, we are already seeing the growth of new and interesting applications utilizing AR. An AR application (Pocket Patrol) is being piloted in Queensland, Australia to provide safety instruction to beach-goers. AR is already an education game-changer, with applications to help students learn anat-

---

[1] A user may operate Pokémon GO in background mode if she has paired it with the Pokémon GO Plus wristband peripheral device made available by Nintendo. More information about that device is available here: *http://www.pokemongo.com/es-es/pokemon-go-plus/*. When the user starts Pokémon GO using the device, she can play even when the app is running in the background, and it collects data in the same fashion as during normal game play.

omy, chemistry, math, and art. For example, the British Museum offers an AR scavenger hunt for kids to collect words and digital objects to solve puzzles as they scan specific exhibition objects with a mobile device. The Smithsonian Museum of Natural History here in Washington has a mobile app that overlays skin onto dinosaur skeletons when kids hold a mobile device over the bones.

AR is also increasingly becoming an important life-saving and ·enhancing tool for public safety and first responders, and will be of even greater use as a dedicated mobile broadband network is built for the public safety and first responder communities.

For us at Niantic, seeing how the public has responded to Field Trip, Ingress and Pokémon GO inspires us to move forward to create and innovate, so we can continue to chase our imaginations. Similarly, it remains important for policy leaders like yourselves to have public policy keep pace with innovation. Properly utilized, public policy can play a central role in driving innovation as it has in Silicon Valley for the past forty years through government-led research and development in fields such as semiconductors, aerospace, and the Internet.

Think of it, a mere 14 years ago, a mobile, augmented reality program required twenty-six pounds of equipment. Today, we can make it work with a smartphone that weighs a little less than half a pound. We at Niantic look forward to what the next fourteen years will bring to this amazing technology.

Thank you, again, Mr. Chairman and Senator Nelson, and I look forward to answering your questions, and more important, working with you to advance public policies that will further advance augmented reality.

The CHAIRMAN. Thank you, Mr. Hanke.
Mr. Mullins?

STATEMENT OF BRIAN MULLINS, CHIEF EXECUTIVE OFFICER, DAQRI

Mr. MULLINS. Chairman Thune, Ranking Member Nelson, and members of the Committee, thank you for the opportunity to speak to you on this important topic. My name is Brian Mullins. I'm the founder and CEO of DAQRI, a Los Angeles-based technology company focused on empowering people with augmented reality. In these brief remarks, I'll discuss the power of AR, how it is being applied today, and why it represents a shift in technology so significant as to rival that of the Internet itself.

I first started working with the technologies that would become AR after graduating from the U.S. Merchant Marine Academy in 1997 and working at the Department of Transportation and later at the Space and Naval Warfare Systems Command. When I left the government sector and moved into the field of industrial automation and robotics, I learned firsthand how technology could dramatically increase workplace efficiency, but was dismayed to see workers left behind as factory floors were transformed. We needed to leverage technology not just to optimize factories, but also to empower the human beings that ran them.

This year, much attention has been focused on AR in the entertainment sector. But behind the scenes, less covered by the media, practical and valuable applications of augmented reality that will positively influence American lives are already gaining momentum in other fields. Industry leaders, such as General Electric, Boeing, Intel, Huntington Ingalls, and countless others, are applying augmented reality in training, maintenance, quality control, remote expert assistance, construction, defense, and manufacturing applications, just to name a few.

Imagine a worker who wants to transition to a new manufacturing facility but lacks formal training for a highly skilled manufacturing role. With AR, they can learn and execute complex tasks, improve productivity, and quickly gain skills and knowledge even in new environments. On the first day at a new factory, AR can show step-by-step instructions on top of the disassembled wing of an aircraft, showing a worker visually how things need to be put together.

This is no longer just a hypothetical scenario. AR technology is already being used to close the skill gap in the workforce, the benefits of which are now supported by industry and academic studies. In 2015, Boeing and Iowa State University published a study comparing the efficacy of traditional work instructions with augmented reality work instructions for aircraft wingtip assembly. While I would refer you to my written testimony and the study itself for specific details, the researchers found that the AR instructions enabled workers to complete tasks significantly faster, more accurately, and with greater enjoyment.

Technology can take away jobs. It's true, though, that most times when it does, it creates new, even better jobs. But, unfortunately, this doesn't happen overnight. It can take years, and an entire segment of workers can be left in the cold trying to reskill when their industry or vocation is no longer relevant. Augmented reality helps people to learn and adapt to new technologies faster than ever before. It empowers workers with an entirely new tool that enables them to keep up with the accelerating pace of change in the modern world.

Analysts predict that sales will grow from $2 billion today to over $100 billion by 2022 across both consumer and enterprise markets. This hearing is timely, because this transition to consumer use is already underway with AR applications in cars. Head-up Displays, a technology developed for fighter pilots to get the information they need in the cockpit without distracting them from their mission, is finding itself on the road today.

The use of HUD in automobiles has been studied extensively and has been shown to have a number of significant safety benefits, the most important of which is enabling the driver of the vehicle to maintain their gaze on the road. You no longer have to look down to see your speedometer or turn-by-turn directions. That information is available at a glance directly in your field of view. DAQRI's own AR technology can already be found in hundreds of thousands of vehicles on the road today, and the market for AR in cars is expected to grow to over 10 million vehicles per year by 2022.

From the beginning of my career, I knew there was something special about a technology that centered on people, allowing humans to adapt to changes in technology as quickly as computers. As AR continues to emerge as one of the most important technologies of the modern world, I ask the Committee to consider the potential AR has to enhance the American worker and create new jobs and opportunities. The use case with consumers will be materially different than the use case in industrial and automotive, and regulations need to be tailored instead of painted with a broad brush.

I applaud the Commerce Committee for their foresight in holding this hearing. I look forward to working with you to help support the emergence of this technology, and I welcome any questions you may have.

[The prepared statement of Mr. Mullins follows:]

PREPARED STATEMENT OF BRIAN MULLINS, CHIEF EXECUTIVE OFFICER, DAQRI

Chairman Thune, Ranking Member Nelson, and members of the Committee, thank you for the opportunity to speak to you on this important topic.

My name is Brian Mullins. I am the founder and CEO of DAQRI, a Los Angeles-based technology company focused on empowering people in our everyday lives through Augmented Reality (AR). In these brief remarks, I will discuss the power of AR, how it is being applied today, and why it represents a shift in technology so significant as to rival that of the Internet itself.

I first started working with AR technologies in 1997 when I started my career at the Department of Transportation (DOT) after graduating from the U.S. Merchant Marine Academy at Kings Point, New York. First at the DOT and later at the Space and Naval Warfare Systems Command, I worked with simulation and early mixed reality technologies that provided a glimpse of what AR would one day become. The technology was early, but I already knew then that it would become the best way to transfer knowledge while maintaining situational awareness.

When I left the government sector and moved into the field of Industrial Automation and Robotics, I learned firsthand how technology could dramatically increase workplace efficiency, but was dismayed to see workers left behind as factory floors were transformed. Drawing upon my earlier experiences, I realized that Augmented Reality could give people the ability to keep pace with the advancement of automation technologies and remain an invaluable part of the loop. We needed to leverage technology not just to optimize factories, but also to empower the human beings that ran them.

This year, much attention has been focused on AR in the entertainment sector. But behind the scenes—less covered by the media—practical and valuable applications of Augmented Reality that will positively influence American lives are already gaining momentum in other fields.

AR is similar to Virtual Reality (VR), but while VR is limited to interactions within a completely virtual world, AR mixes the real and the virtual together, allowing you to enhance what you see, without losing the connection to the world around you.

Today, AR technology allows you to overlay information into the real world and rapidly transfer knowledge that empowers people to make decisions that would not be possible without it. Augmented Reality devices will have a significant impact in the workplace. Gartner's 2016 forecast cites these business drivers for wearable head-up displays:[1] hands free worker productivity and safety, training in simulated environments, checklists for quality control, real-time training, and remote expert assistance and collaboration.

Industry leaders such as General Electric, Boeing, Intel, Huntington Ingalls, and countless others are applying Augmented Reality in training, maintenance, operations, construction, defense and manufacturing applications. The use of AR in the enterprise can also reduce errors, increase efficiency on complex tasks, and contribute to significant improvements in worker safety.

Imagine a worker who wants to transition to a new manufacturing facility that opened in her community, but lacks formal training for a highly skilled manufacturing role. Through the power of AR, she can be empowered to learn and execute complex tasks, improve productivity, and quickly gain new skills and knowledge even in environments where she has little experience through guided, step-by-step, augmented reality work instructions. On her first day at a new factory, using AR, she can look at the disassembled wing of an aircraft and see step by step instructions right on top of the components that she needs to put together.

This is not a hypothetical scenario. In 2015, Boeing and Iowa State University published a study [2] comparing the efficacy of traditional desktop work instructions with augmented reality work instructions for aircraft wingtip assembly. The team observed first-time trainees doing complex manufacturing tasks, and tracked a few key productivity stats. Major increases in efficiency, accuracy, speed, and worker satisfaction were found. Here are some highlights:

- *Accuracy:* Trainees utilizing AR instructions made fewer errors than those using desktop instructions by a factor of 16-to-1 on the trainees' first time completing

---

[1] Gartner Forecast: Wearable Electronic Devices, Worldwide, 2016, Analyst(s): Angela McIntyre, Brian Blau, Michele Reitz

[2] Fusing Self-Reported and Sensor Data from Mixed-Reality Training, *(I/ITSEC) 2014, Trevor Richardson, Stephen Gilbert, Joseph Holub, Frederick Thompson, Anastacia MacAllister, Rafael Radkowski, Eliot Winer Iowa State University, Paul Davies, Scott Terry, The Boeing Company*

a task. On the second time around, those using AR had perfect performance—zero errors. Overall, the AR work instructions improved first time quality by 94 percent.

- *Speed:* Trainees using AR instructions were able to complete tasks significantly faster than their counterparts, reducing job completion time by an average of 30 percent and, in some cases, as much as 50 percent.
- *Greater focus:* AR allowed workers to maintain focus on the task at hand. Trainees using AR looked at their instructions less frequently and for shorter periods of time, demonstrating that comprehension was happening rapidly. As the team put it, "The fewer number of looks meant that participants were not 'bouncing' back and forth between the instructions and the physical task."
- *Satisfied workers:* How did workers feel about the experience? A post-action survey asked participants if they would agree with the statement, "I would recommend work instructions like this to a friend." The answer was a resounding "Yes," at rates roughly 4 times higher than the median score for questions like this at more than 400 companies in 28 industries.

The AR instructions in this study enabled workers to complete tasks faster, more accurately and with greater enjoyment. Such results promise improved outcomes for industrial businesses, while also enhancing quality of life for workers.

Technology can take away jobs. It's true though that most times when it does, it creates new, even better jobs. But this doesn't happen overnight. It can take years, and an entire segment of workers can be left in the cold trying to re-skill when their industry or vocation is no longer relevant. Augmented Reality is a technology that helps people to learn and adapt to new technologies faster than ever before. It empowers workers with an entirely new tool that enables them to keep up with the accelerating pace of change in the modern world.

This year consumer awareness of AR is higher than ever thanks to the rise in gaming applications kicked off by the Pokémon Go phenomenon, however the adoption of AR has already been underway in the enterprise market for some time. Analysts predict that sales will grow from $2B today to over $100B by 2022 in combined hardware and software, across both consumer and enterprise markets.

Much like cellular phone technology, I expect AR to continue to develop in the enterprise market before it moves to consumers. And as it does, it will enter our day to day lives in a way that we haven't yet discussed. This hearing is timely because this transition to consumer use is already underway with AR Applications in cars.

Automotive Head-up Displays (HUD), a technology developed for fighter pilots to get the information they need in the cockpit without distracting them from their mission is finding itself on the road today.

DAQRI's own AR technology can already be found in hundreds of thousands of vehicles on the road today, providing drivers with critical information in the windscreen, reducing distraction and helping drivers to make decisions faster. At the current rate of growth, the market for AR in cars is expected to grow to over 10 million vehicles per year by 2022.

With a HUD you no longer have to look down to see your speedometer, that information is available at a glance, directly in your field of view. AR technology is making driving safer by providing information like turn by turn directions directly on top of the road. When information is in the space around us, it is more intuitive and easier to understand.

The use of HUD in automobiles has been studied extensively [3,4] and has been shown to have a number of significant safety benefits, the most important of which is enabling the driver of the vehicle to maintain their gaze on the road. This reduces the "blind flight" time, which can equate to a significant distance when travelling at speed. Because of this, it is anticipated that the number of vehicles fitted with Head Up Displays at build time will increase significantly in the near future.

And now, as cars become more intelligent there is an even greater need for information to flow to the driver. A driver assist system can communicate to the driver that there is a hazard ahead they might not have seen, or perhaps a self-driving car will inform the passengers that it is aware of the truck that moved in front of them, and that it will be taking action accordingly. A visual connection between the

---

[3] N. J. Ward and A. Parkes, "Head-up displays and their automotive application: An overview of human factors issues affecting safety," *Accident Analysis & Prevention,* vol. 26, no. 6, pp. 703–717, 1994.

[4] R. J. Kiefer and A. W. Gellatly, "Quantifying t he Consequences of the 'Eyes-on-Road' Benefit Attributed to Head-Up Displays," p. 960946, Feb. 1996.

vehicle and the driver using AR is one of the most powerful ways to improve safety on the road today.

From the beginning of my career, I knew there was something special about a technology that centered around people and allowing humans to adapt to changes in technology as quickly as computers. I am honored to stand before you and share the amazing possibilities that AR has to enhance the American worker and create new jobs and opportunities that will fundamentally make a positive impact on the world in years to come.

As AR continues to emerge as one of the most important technologies of the modern world, I ask the Committee to consider the transformational impact that this technology has on our society. The use case with consumers will be materially different than the use case in the industrial environment and regulations to support that need to be tailored instead of painted with a broad brush.

I applaud the Commerce Committee for their foresight in holding this hearing now to begin to understand these issues and I look forward to partnering with the United States Government to help support the emergence of this transformational technology.

Figure 1: Augmented Reality Work Instructions

Figure 2: Automotive Augmented Reality

52

The CHAIRMAN. Thank you very much, Mr. Mullins.
Mr. Pierre-Louis?

**STATEMENT OF STANLEY PIERRE-LOUIS,
SENIOR VICE PRESIDENT AND GENERAL COUNSEL,
ENTERTAINMENT SOFTWARE ASSOCIATION**

Mr. PIERRE-LOUIS. Chairman Thune, Ranking Member Nelson, distinguished members of the Committee, we are honored to be invited to testify about the exciting developing technologies that will transform the way our consumers engage with our content. I am Stanley Pierre-Louis, and I serve as Senior Vice President and General Counsel of the Entertainment Software Association.

ESA is dedicated to serving the policy and public affairs needs of companies that publish computer and video games for video game consoles, handheld devices, personal computers, and the Internet. Our members are at the forefront of the ongoing technological revolution in interactive entertainment.

It is important to note, however, that the technologies that we are addressing today will have applications that stretch well beyond the video game industry and beyond the entertainment sector more broadly. They will impact sectors as varied as education, healthcare, engineering, architecture, and national defense, just to name a few.

My written testimony delves into the distinctions between augmented reality, mixed reality, and virtual reality. Today's other panelists are more expert than I am in these areas, so I will focus my oral testimony on the legal considerations arising out of these new technologies and our industry's approach to addressing them.

As technologies have emerged over time, laws have developed and evolved to ensure Americans' privacy and data security. Our Federal laws and regulations have proven to be sufficiently robust to protect consumer interests, while remaining flexible enough to allow industries to innovate and deliver products and services to customers specified to their needs. And in the states and territories, there's no shortage of statutory and common laws governing negligence, trespass, privacy, data protection, and product liability.

ESA members are committed to meaningful privacy and data security protections and to providing the tools consumers need to make informed decisions about the products they plan to buy. Our industry has embraced a culture of self-regulation and informed consent. To that end, our industry has long adopted practices that go well beyond what is required by law to inform consumers about our products and privacy practices.

In 1994, for example, our industry created the Entertainment Software Rating Board, a nonprofit, self-regulatory body that assigns ratings for games and apps so parents can make informed choices. The ESRB rating system encompasses guidance about age appropriateness, content, and the interactive elements. This program has been lauded by the Federal Trade Commission for our industry's compliance with the program as well as for providing conspicuous, straightforward, and informative disclosures to consumers. More importantly, this program has served its ultimate purpose, as consumers report being highly aware of the ratings of the products we sell.

Since 1999, our industry has also operated the Privacy Certified Program, which provides online privacy solutions to address the growing complexity of privacy protection laws. Among other things, the Privacy Certified Program enjoys a safe harbor status which shields program members from potential sanctions or fines from the FTC and from state attorneys general when violations of COPPA or other state legislation arise.

When it comes to balancing children's welfare, parental responsibility, and the freedom of expression, the technology behind augmented reality and mixed reality fit neatly within these existing legal frameworks. After all, these are technologies that, at their core, are advanced content delivery systems.

Just five years ago, the U.S. Supreme Court recognized in *Brown* v. *Entertainment Merchants Association* that video games are express works that enjoy the same First Amendment protections as books, plays, and movies. And as the late Justice Antonin Scalia aptly explained in his majority opinion, "whatever the challenges of applying the Constitution to ever-advancing technology, 'the basic principles of freedom of speech and the press, like the First Amendment's command, do not vary' when a new and different medium for communication appears."

The Court rejected the argument that video games present special problems because they are interactive, noting that interactivity has always been a feature and a goal of expressive works. In effect, the Supreme Court left little doubt that our foundational laws governing speech are well equipped to address emerging technologies like augmented reality and mixed reality.

We encourage the Committee to give these technologies the space they need to grow and to avoid any redundant and unnecessary regulation that would have a chilling effect on this nascent and promising industry.

Thank you again for the opportunity to testify today about the thrilling new technological developments underway. We look forward to working with the Committee and answering any questions you may have.

[The prepared statement of Mr. Pierre-Louis follows:]

PREPARED STATEMENT OF STANLEY PIERRE-LOUIS, SENIOR VICE PRESIDENT AND GENERAL COUNSEL, ENTERTAINMENT SOFTWARE ASSOCIATION

Chairman Thune, Ranking Member Nelson, distinguished Members of the Committee, my name is Stanley Pierre-Louis, and I am Senior Vice President and General Counsel of the Entertainment Software Association ("ESA"). Thank you for inviting me to testify today. ESA is dedicated to serving the policy and public affairs needs of companies that publish computer and video games for video game consoles, handheld devices, personal computers and the Internet. Our members employ highly-skilled artists, authors, software programmers, engineers and developers who produce a wide array of highly-expressive, interactive works, which include audiovisual materials, musical compositions, literary works, artistic works and software. Last year alone, the video game industry generated more than $23 billion in revenue in the United States and entertained hundreds of millions of consumers throughout the world. Our members are at the forefront of the ongoing technological revolution in interactive entertainment, and I am honored to be invited to testify today about the exciting developing technologies known as Augmented Reality (or "AR") and Mixed Reality (or "MR").

I. Introduction

AR and MR have some similarities to their better-known cousin, Virtual Reality (or "VR"), but differ in key respects—mainly, how the video graphics and digital content integrate with the physical world around us. With *Virtual Reality,* the user typically wears a headset or opaque goggles (often accompanied by headphones) and is closed off from the "real world." The user is fully immersed in a software-generated environment (often termed a "virtual world") displayed before her eyes. By contrast, *Augmented Reality* involves computer technology that overlays software-generated images, sounds and other information over the "real world." Complementary hardware for AR can include a visor with transparent (or semi-transparent) lenses, a head-mounted display, or a hand-held device, such as a smart phone or video game equipment. *Pokémon GO,* the mobile game that captured the attention of millions of users worldwide this summer, is one of the best-known examples of AR. That game was released on July 6, 2016, and, within a week, as many as twen- ty-five million U.S. smartphones had logged in to play the game.[1]

Because AR can be used to overlay data on top of "real world" activities, it is versatile in a variety of contexts. One popular use of AR technology occurs in broadcasts of National Football League games, where a virtual blue line is overlaid across the field to represent the "line of scrimmage" and a virtual yellow line is overlaid across the field to represent the "first down" marker.[2] Earlier uses of this technology were simulated in several scenes of the 1977 epic film *Star Wars: Episode IV—A New Hope,* including when Princess Leia sent a pivotal holographic message to General Obi-Wan Kenobi.[3]

The potential for AR is enormous. Imagine walking through an airport and seeing personalized directions to your gate; watching a city bus approach and knowing immediately whether it is the bus you need or how long you will need to wait for the next bus; walking by a restaurant that prompts a menu to "float" in front of you; or getting turn-by-turn instructions on your windshield while driving.[4]

Mixed Reality contains elements of both VR and AR. Whereas VR immerses you in a simulated world—and whereas AR overlays digital information in real-world settings—MR blends 3–D digital content into your physical world. Using a transparent lens or goggles, the user can see *both* the real world *and* a virtual world seamlessly tied together. MR differs from AR in that the virtual images and elements overlaid in the user's field of vision can interact with and recognize the user and are spatially aware of the environment. In MR, virtual objects placed in the real world appear real and tangible to the user. The user is allowed to move those objects around, observe their minute details, and even interact with them using gestures or voice commands. Imagine hiking on a nature trail with a virtual companion who cannot only tell you where to go, but teach you about your surroundings.[5] Or, in the video game context, imagine defending against a virtual army of flying robots that have invaded your home through the living room walls.[6] The possibilities of these new technologies are truly limitless.

In many ways, VR, AR and MR are *evolutionary:* they emerged from advancements in existing technologies, such as microchip processing, software, razor display screens, GPS, 3–D graphics, wearable computers and the mobile Internet. Legal frameworks developed in the context of these related technologies have protected the public interest throughout those advancements.

But, these technologies may also prove to be *revolutionary.* We may not yet have George Jetson's flying car, but we do have AR and MR. It is no longer science fiction. The public's excitement over the entertainment possibilities of VR, MR and AR may be driving the current wave of innovation and pushing products to market, but we are only beginning to scratch the surface of what these technologies can achieve. Indeed, the possibilities for the application of these technologies in the fields of education, healthcare; science, business and national defense are bountiful. And, they will become more interactive, more immersive and more accessible and more afford-

---

[1] *Future Reality: Virtual, Augmented & Mixed Reality (VR, AR, & MR) Primer,* Bank of America Merrill Lynch Thematic Investing, Sept. 7, 2016, at 41 [hereinafter "Bank of America Report"].

[2] Brian D. Wassom, *Augmented Reality Law, Privacy, and Ethics: Law, Society, and Emerging AR Technologies,* at 7 (Allison Bishop ed., Syngress, 2015).

[3] See *http://www.starwars.com/video/help-me-obi-wan-kenobi* (video of holographic message from Princess Leia).

[4] Ian King and Dana Hull, *The Car Windshield is Turning into a Computer Screen,* Bloomberg (Jan. 22, 2015), *https://www.bloomberg.com/news/articles/2015-01-22/the-car-windshield-is-turning-into-a-computer-screen.*

[5] To be sure, several mobile apps already provide hikers with trail directions and information about their surroundings. See *http://beyond.com/blog/how-augmented-reality-will-make-you-a-smart-hiker/* (discussing the use of AR in hiking apps); see also *http://www.atlasandboots.com/best-hiking-apps/* (listing mobile and AR hiking apps). However, as MR capabilities advance, the technology will become more integrated into the user experience.

[6] See *RoboRaid* video, available at *https://www.microsoft.com/microsoft-hololens/en-us/apps/roboraid.*

able over time. Goldman Sachs researchers recently estimated that, by 2025, VR and AR will constitute at least a $23 billion market and could even be as much as a $182 billion market.[7]

American technologists and entrepreneurs are leading the way, just as they did at the dawn of the Internet. Our members are at the forefront of this innovation, but they are by no means alone. As with past technological leaps, the government should embrace and empower these emerging technologies by allowing them to iterate, grow and flourish so they can reach their full potential benefit to the American society and economy. I am pleased to be here today to talk about the applications emerging in this field, as well as a few of the ongoing considerations that are at the forefront of this evolution.

II. Current and Predicted Applications of these Emerging Technologies

AR and MR technologies already offer immersive game-playing and entertainment experiences. Some examples include using video game controllers to play air hockey on a virtual field that is projected by the light bars on the controllers (*The Playroom,* Sony PlayStation 4); solving a high-tech crime thriller that uses objects in your physical space to create the crime scene and for hiding clues (*Fragments,* Microsoft HoloLens); and a fighting dragon that pops up from an AR playing card (*Archery,* Nintendo 3DS). However, in addition to providing entertainment, these technologies will likely serve more broadly as platforms for our routine daily tasks. Think of the smartphone. This one device, which emanated from the mobile phone, now serves as an e-mail and texting hub, a calendar, a to-do list, a health monitor, a map, a music player, a weather forecaster and a ride-hailing service, to name just a few applications. AR and MR have the potential to fuel the next generation of tools to make our daily lives even more productive and enjoyable and to connect people who might be miles apart. They are poised to dramatically improve many sectors of our society and economy. Here are just a few of the sectors that stand to be dramatically improved by AR and MR.

In the *Entertainment* sector, content creators and consumers are teeming with excitement over AR and MR.[8] Video games have already undergone dramatic improvements in user experience, but AR and MR present new possibilities. And, as the recent success of *Pokémon GO* suggests, this evolution can have ancillary societal benefits. For example, unlike traditional video games that were best played from the living room or on PCs, AR and MR experiences can be suited to a variety of locations, both indoors and out. *Pokémon GO* motivates users to explore the real world around them: to go outdoors and be active. This new and promising evolution of games integrates learning, exploration and physical activity like never before.

For video entertainment, AR and MR will be used by artists to imagine and bring new worlds to life and to augment our existing worlds in ways that once seemed impossible. Peter Jackson, the Oscar-winning director of the *Lord of the Rings* series, serves on the advisory panel for Magic Leap, one of ESA's member companies that is at the forefront of developing MR technology. Jackson recently told *Wired* magazine, "[t]his mixed reality is not an extension of 3–D movies. It's something completely different. . . . Once you can create the illusion of solid objects anywhere you want, you create new entertainment opportunities."[9]

Indeed, Magic Leap's MR technology is nothing short of amazing; it creates "mixed-reality objects" that "are aware of their environment." [10] Advanced hardware "constantly gathers information, scanning the room for obstacles, listening for voices, tracking eye movements and watching hands." [11]

Healthcare. AR and MR may prove transformative to the healthcare industry. Already today, AR is being used to address the pain management and rehabilitation

---

[7] Heather Bellini *et al., Virtual & Augmented Reality: Understanding the Race for the Next Computing Platform,* Goldman Sachs Global Investment Research, Jan. 13, 2016, at 14 [hereinafter "Goldman Sachs Report"].

[8] John Gaudiosi, *Why Gamers are Excited about Virtual Reality and Augmented Reality,* Fortune (Sept. 11, 2015), *http://fortune.com/2015/09/11/gamers-are-excited-about-vr-ar/* ("Gamers are always looking to the next thing, whether it is the next game in a franchise or the next hardware platform/capability.").

[9] Kevin Kelly, *The Untold Story of Magic Leap, the World's Most Secretive Startup,* Wired (April 2016), *https://www.wired.com/2016/04/magic-leap-vr/.*

[10] David M. Ewalt, *Inside Magic Leap, The Secretive $4.5 Billion Startup Changing Computing Forever,* Forbes (Nov. 2, 2016), *http://www.forbes.com/sites/davidewalt/2016/11/02/inside-magic-leap-the-secretive-4-5-billion-startup-changing-computing-forever/#491fca29e83f.*

[11] *Id.*

needs of pediatric burn victims.[12] In the future, one could imagine a surgeon wearing AR or MR glasses to review a patient's MRI scan results while the scan is overlaid on top of the patient. There may be therapeutic uses as well; patients experiencing pain could be transported to relaxing destinations. Some researchers are even testing the ability of VR to help paraplegics learn to walk again.[13] And still other researchers are examining whether these technologies can help treat patients with phobias or PTSD, as "virtual worlds can create artificial, controlled stimuli in order to habituate the patient to those environments that cause anxiety." [14]

Education. The applications of these technologies to education are endless. For example, Microsoft has worked with Case Western Reserve University to use the HoloLens for medical student training; medical students can view and interact with a holographic human body with animated skeletal structure and circulatory system, replacing the need for cadavers.[15] Microsoft is also working with the educational publisher Pearson to use the HoloLens to create a number of learning tools, including online tutoring and coaching in areas as disparate as nursing, engineering and construction.[16]

Today, users can download iPhone apps that identify stars, constellations and satellites when users direct their iPhones to the night sky.[17] However, one can also imagine a class learning about the Civil War and seeing a three-dimensional representation of Abraham Lincoln standing before the students, delivering the Gettysburg Address. And, one can imagine students being virtually transported to the Colosseum in Rome during the Flavian dynasty to experience life as a gladiator. According to a professor of education the University of Pennsylvania's Graduate School of Education, "[r]esearch shows that interacting with AR alone improves students' understanding of a concept." [18]

In addition, high-risk professionals would be able to receive realistic, hands-on training in a safe environment. AR and MR technology will enabling users to tour a new city and immediately learn background information about monuments or architecturally significant buildings simply by looking at them. And, one day, we might really know what it is like to stand in another's shoes, walking through simulations designed to help us understand each other better to help foster empathy.[19]

Business and Engineering. As previously mentioned, Microsoft is already selling its MR visor, called HoloLens, to developers. A user of the HoloLens will be able to watch "a live football game on a virtual screen 'hovering' next to a web browser window, alongside a few other virtual screens." [20] These "hovering" screens could eventually replace the various physical screens we use today at home and at the office because they can be summoned into (and out of) your field of vision and pinned to the walls and counters of your physical space as requested while using AR and MR glasses. The mix of entertainment, information and work applications has the potential to improve every workspace in America.

The applications for architects, builders, designers, artists and engineers will be nothing short of transformative. Instead of looking at a two-dimensional computer screen rendering a space in 3–D, users will be able to stand in the space as they create it before a single brick is laid. In fact, Lockheed Martin has collaborated on AR projects to speed up the maintenance process for F–22 and F–35 fighter jets:

---

[12]Jonathan Mott, *et al.*, *The Efficacy of an Augmented Virtual Reality System to Alleviate Pain in Children Undergoing Burns Dressing Changes: A Randomised Controlled Trial*, Burns Journal (September 2008), *http://www.burnsjournal.com/article/S0305-4179(07)00286-0/abstract*; Monika Joshi, *Pokémon Go Helps Harborview Patients Heal*, America's Essential Hospitals (Aug. 11, 2016), *https://essentialhospitals.org/pokemon-go-helps-patients-heal/*.

[13] Ananya Bhattacharya, *Paraplegics are Learning to Walk Again with Virtual Reality*, Quartz (Aug. 15, 2016), *http://qz.com/757516/paraplegics-are-learning-to-walk-again-with-virtual-reality/*.

[14]Goldman Sachs Report at 24.

[15] Kathryn Jeffords, *Virtual and Augmented Reality: Changing the Game in Healthcare*, Science Media Awards Summit in the Hub (June 29, 2016), *http://www.sciencemediasummit.org/blog/virtual-and-augmented-reality-changing-the-game-in-healthcare*.

[16]Mark Coppock, *Microsoft and Pearson are partnering to Turn HoloLens into an Educational Tool*, Digital Trends (Oct. 26, 2016), *http://www.digitaltrends.com/computing/pearson-hololens-mixed-reality-education/*.

[17] Ci, *5 Superb Augmented Reality Astronomy Apps for iPhone*, iPhoneness (June 17, 2016), *http://www.iphoneness.com/iphone-apps/augmented-reality-astronomy-apps/*.

[18] Susan A. Yoon, *The Educator's Playbook: The Role of Augmented Reality in a Lesson Plan*, Penn GSE Newsroom (2016), *http://www.gse.upenn.edu/news/educators-playbook/role-augmented-reality-lesson-plan*.

[19]Nick Harley, *How Augmented Reality and Empathetic Storytelling is Changing Audience Engagement*, PR Newswire for Journalists (Aug. 31, 2016), *https://mediablog.prnewswire.com/2016/08/31/how-augmented-reality-and-empathetic-storytelling-is-changing-audience-engagement/*.

[20]Kelly, *supra* note 9.

"When an engineer looks at the aircraft using the smart glasses, they see digitally displayed plans projected over the physical plane. They can then use a tablet to enter any damage or defects." [21]

This technology also enhances the ability of consumers to become more mobile. Have a new job in St. Louis or in Tampa? Instead of incurring the expense of flying to look for a new home, take a virtual tour of homes from right where you are.[22] Similarly, vacationers are now able to explore possible destinations before committing to a locale or a hotel.[23]

National Defense. The United States military already uses VR to train military personnel, including flight and combat simulations.[24] As this technology helps create more realistic, immersive simulations, this aspect of military training will become increasingly useful and effective. It is also not hard to imagine the value of AR or MR glasses on the battlefield, where vital information could be placed strategically in the user's field of vision, accessible without the user having to resort to looking down at a screen or map. Indeed, so-called "heads-up" displays are now commonplace in our military's advanced fighter jets.[25]

III. Legal Landscape

As technologies have emerged over time, laws have developed and evolved to ensure Americans' privacy and data security. Our Federal laws and regulations have proven to be sufficiently robust to protect consumer interests, while remaining flexible enough to allow industries to innovate and deliver products and services to customers specified to their needs. Moreover, in each state and territory, there is no shortage of statutory and common laws governing negligence, trespass, privacy, data protection and product liability.

ESA's members are committed to meaningful privacy and data security protections and to providing the tools consumers need to make informed decisions about the products they plan to purchase. Our industry has embraced a culture of self-regulation and "informed consent." To that end, our industry has long adopted practices that go well beyond what is required by law to inform consumers about our products and privacy practices. In 1994, for example, our industry created the Entertainment Software Rating Board ("ESRB"), a non-profit, self-regulatory body that assigns ratings for video games and apps so parents can make informed choices. The ESRB rating system encompasses guidance about age-appropriateness, content, and interactive elements.[26] This program has been lauded by the Federal Trade Commission ("FTC") for our industry's compliance with the program as well as for providing conspicuous, straightforward and informative disclosures to consumers.[27] More importantly, this program has served its ultimate purpose, as our consumers are highly aware of the ratings of the products we sell.[28]

Since 1999, the ESRB has also operated the *Privacy Certified* program (formerly the *ESRB Privacy Online* program), which provides online privacy solutions to address the growing complexity of privacy protection laws. Among other things, the *Privacy Certified* program enjoys "safe harbor" status, which shields program members from potential sanctions or fines from the FTC and/or state attorneys general when violations of the Children's Online Privacy Protection Act (or similar state legislation) arise.[29]

When it comes to balancing children's welfare, parental responsibility and the freedom of speech and expression, AR and MR technologies fit neatly within existing

---

[21] See *Augmented Reality and Workplace Training*, SpongeUK (June 19, 2015), *http://spongeuk.com/2015/06/augmented-reality-and-workplace-training/*.

[22] See *https://www.vrglobal.com/real-estate/* (solutions for virtual tours using VR and AR technologies).

[23] See *http://www.augment.com/blog/augmented-reality-in-tourism/*, (discussing use of AR technology in tourism).

[24] Goldman Sachs Report at 26.

[25] See Sean Gallagher, *"Magic Helmet" for F–35 ready for delivery*, Ars Technica (July 24, 2014), *http://arstechnica.com/information-technology/2014/07/magic-helmet-for-f-35-ready-for-delivery/*.

[26] In 2015, ESRB expanded the use of its ratings to mobile and digital storefronts as part of the International Age Rating Coalition ("IARC"). Information on IARC available at: *https://www.globalratings.com/*.

[27] See *FTC Undercover Shopper Survey on Entertainment Ratings Enforcement Finds Compliance Highest Among Video Game Sellers and Movie Theaters*, FTC (March 25, 2013), *https://www.ftc.gov/news-events/press-releases/2013/03/ftc-undercover-shopper-survey-entertainment-ratings-enforcement*.

[28] See *ESRB Survey: Parental Awareness and Use*, *https://www.esrb.org/about/awareness.aspx* ("86 percent of parents are aware of the ESRB rating system").

[29] For more information on the ESRB *Privacy Certified* program, see *https://www.esrb.org/privacy/faq.aspx#2*.

legal frameworks. After all, AR and MR are, at their core, advanced content delivery systems. Just five years ago, the U.S. Supreme Court recognized in *Brown v. Entertainment Merchants Association* that video games are expressive works that enjoy the same First Amendment protections as "books, plays, and movies." [30] As the late Justice Antonin Scalia aptly explained in his majority opinion, "whatever the challenges of applying the Constitution to ever-advancing technology, 'the basic principles of freedom of speech and the press, like the First Amendment's command, do not vary' when a new and different medium for communication appears." [31] The Court rejected the argument that "video games present special problems because they are 'interactive,' " noting that "interactivity" has always been a feature—and a goal—of expressive works: "the better it is, the more interactive." [32] The Supreme Court left little doubt that our foundational laws governing speech are well-equipped to address emerging technologies like AR and MR.

History is instructive on other examples of the law's adaptability to new technologies. In the late 1990s, during the still-early days of the World Wide Web, the FTC believed that many Internet sites did not provide consumers with adequate disclosures.[33] The FTC responded by developing guidance (known as the "Dot Com Disclosures") to help businesses apply established principles of "clear and conspicuous" disclosure to the online context. It has since updated that guidance several times as the Internet has evolved.[34] All of this has occurred within existing FTC authority and without the need to amend the FTC Act.[35]

We encourage the Committee to give AR and MR the space they need to grow, and to avoid any redundant and unnecessary regulation that would have a chilling effect on this nascent and promising industry.

IV. Conclusion

Thank you again for the opportunity to testify today about the thrilling new technological developments under way. These are exciting times for creators, developers, consumers and our country as a whole. AR and MR have tremendous potential beyond entertainment. We should encourage continued American innovation and investment in these areas. And when issues arise, we should look first to existing legal frameworks that have served consumers well in the past. We look forward to working with the Committee and answering any questions you might have.

The CHAIRMAN. Thank you, Mr. Pierre-Louis.

We'll proceed to questions, I think.

Senator Nelson, do you want to submit, or do you want to make a statement?

STATEMENT OF HON. BILL NELSON, U.S. SENATOR FROM FLORIDA

Senator NELSON. Mr. Chairman, you're very kind. I'll submit an opening statement.

[The prepared statement of Senator Nelson follows:]

PREPARED STATEMENT OF HON. BILL NELSON, U.S. SENATOR FROM FLORIDA

Chairman Thune, thank you for holding this hearing to explore the exciting promises of augmented reality technologies and to spur important discussions on the many policy questions that augmented reality raises.

Over the August recess, I took a tour of Magic Leap's facility in Dania Beach, Florida. Magic Leap, which will be headquartered in Plantation, is one of the leading, cutting-edge AR companies in the world.

---

[30] 564 U.S. 786, 790 (2011).

[31] *Id.*

[32] *Id.* at 798 (internal quotation marks omitted).

[33] See *FTC Staff Issues Guidelines on Internet Advertising* (May 3, 2000), *https://www.ftc.gov/news-events/press-releases/2000/05/ftc-staff-issues-guidelines-internet-advertising.*

[34] See *FTC Staff Revises Online Advertising Disclosure Guidelines* (March 12, 2013), *https://www.ftc.gov/news-events/press-releases/2013/03/ftc-staff-revises-online-advertising-disclosure-guidelines.*

[35] See *.com Disclosures: How to Make Effective Disclosures in Digital Advertising,* FTC (March 2013) at p. 2, *https://www.ftc.gov/system/files/documents/plain-language/bus41-dot-com-disclosures-information-about-online-advertising.pdf* ("The FTC Act's prohibition on 'unfair or deceptive acts or practices' broadly covers advertising claims, marketing and promotional activities, and sale practices in general. The Act is not limited to any particular medium.").

And what I saw was truly amazing—not only because this technology will change how we interact with the world, but also because of what it means for growing Florida's economy and creating well-paying, high-skilled jobs.

And, if I may, Chairman Thune, I'd like to submit for the record a recent piece in *Wired* Magazine on Magic Leap.

Yes, augmented reality can be used for video games. But it can also be used to educate or do business like never before, spurring efficiency and convenience. And the technology has the potential to break down barriers for those with disabilities and create a safer world for consumers.

One of the big questions is: what does augmented reality mean for consumer privacy? AR devices can potentially record, download, and store vast amounts of information about the real world, including about innocent bystanders who may have no clue they are being recorded. What are we going to do to protect their privacy?

And what must be done to make sure that these devices are secure from hackers and cyber-vulnerabilities? For instance, augmented reality is being used in cars so drivers can get real-time information on their windshields. Will hackers be able to infiltrate that system and, say, block the driver's view of a stop sign or a pedestrian crossing the street?

How will we protect children from unsuitable augmented reality content? Parents are already struggling to shield their kids from adult-oriented and dangerous videos and video games. This could be an even bigger problem for parents when it comes to sophisticated AR content that may be completely inappropriate for young eyes and brains.

These are the types of questions I hope our witnesses can shed some light on. I share my colleagues' enthusiasm about this exciting, ground-breaking technology. And I'm a believer in what this growing industry can do for states like mine in creating the jobs of tomorrow. But we also must ask some of the tough questions to make sure that innovation is taking place in a responsible manner.

Thank you.

Senator NELSON. May I just ask one question, because I want to give our other members a chance here.

Cybersecurity—we've seen how you can take over a car. You could possibly take over an airplane. So could a hacker make a digital flock of birds, if you're using AR in the cockpit, to make it look as if it were going to fly through the windshield of the airplane? And what can we do about that?

Mr. MULLINS. Senator, thank you for the question. I think it's a fantastic question. I think as the technology gets better, the simple answer is yes, we could make virtual objects that are indistinguishable from the real world. I think the underlying question about the security of augmented reality is a very serious question that applies to technology in general and is one that we need to get out in front of and plan for in the products we make and as we develop the technologies.

There will certainly be new opportunities with augmented reality for exploitation by bad actors, as there is with any new technology. I think it's questions like this being asked today that will help us get in front of those problems as an industry and in regulation.

Mr. CALO. I just want to add to that. One of the recommendations that we came up with within the Tech Policy Lab—one of my colleagues, who is my co-director of the lab actually did the original work showing that you could take over a car and cause it to break and do all these different things—Tadayoshi Kohno—was that with augmented reality, doing really good threat modeling is critically important. By threat modeling, we mean that you imagine all the things that people might be able to do with it, including—and that's a brilliant one—the idea of introducing a fake flock of birds. But just think, you know, you could also have it happen much more simply, such as just obscuring a stop sign so that you don't see it. I remember that my colleague, Tadayoshi Kohno, had an app that he was using when he was running to keep track of his running, and he looked at it, and he thought that he saw a spider on it. So he threw it to the ground, and it broke. It actually broke his phone.

Later, what we pieced together was that an app that was tracking his running had allowed an exterminator service to take over and do an advertisement, and the advertisement was like a shock advertisement to scare him into thinking it was a—he really got scared. And as a tort professor, that strikes me as being an awful lot like kind of a digital assault.

So I think that when bones instead of bits are on the line, I think that the kind of thing that you're talking about is particularly crucial, and I think that it is absolutely incumbent on these companies to make sure that they're doing very good threat modeling and taking security extremely seriously.

Mr. HANKE. If I could add one thing to that, I'm very glad you raised that question. I absolutely think it's incumbent upon all of us offering products to have best-of-breed security out there. For any company that's trying to operate in today's environment, that is a core part of the business. You have to invest in it. I think we were kind of lucky at Niantic in that we had the benefit of working within Google for many years—many of the core members of the team—which has had to deal with all kinds of threats, and we knew that we were going to have to expect that.

But to the point I made earlier about sometimes it not feeling like there's a sheriff, I would just reemphasize that it's a lot to ask of U.S. companies to go out there when threats can come flying in, and do come flying in, constantly from all over the world, where people essentially can act with impunity, and you stop them in one place, and they come back somewhere else. There's no real risk to this for the folks that are doing it. So we are asking a lot of our companies to play whack-a-mole and to just continuously fight off those attacks on their own.

Senator NELSON. By the way, if you're the guy who developed Google Earth, thank you. I use it all the time, and I use it to see what roads are congested.

[Laughter.]

Mr. HANKE. That's great to hear. Thank you.

Mr. PIERRE-LOUIS. Senator Nelson, Stan Pierre-Louis. In answer to your question, one of the interesting things about being in the video game industry is that we are dual DNA. We are both a content industry, because we create creative works, but we're also a software industry, so we're a tech. So we've got a lot to think about when we put our products out.

One is how do we protect our content—very important—and we've got security measures there both in terms of the software and the consoles or other devices. Second, we need to think about how we protect our corporate data, because that's very valuable and important, and the third is how do we protect consumer data. So the thought process of that protection goes very deep into the design of how we create our works and distribute those works.

But more and more, as you're seeing larger threats and as you're seeing state actors make those threats, one of the areas that obviously has to be taken into consideration is what we do about our cybersecurity laws and strengthening them. That's one of the areas that we think about. How do we strengthen them to make sure that we're all headed toward the same goal and not creating opportunities for bad actors? So that's going to be an important element of this as well.

The CHAIRMAN. Thank you, Senator Nelson. Echo on the Google Earth. I'm a big fan of Google Earth, so well done.

Senator Wicker?

STATEMENT OF HON. ROGER F. WICKER, U.S. SENATOR FROM MISSISSIPPI

Senator WICKER. I'm sorry I didn't get here in time for the demonstrations. But let me ask about what this is going to do for job creation in a state like mine. We'll start with Mr. Mullins.

You've got the Smart Helmet. Is this going to create jobs? Is it going to replace jobs? And in what ways might this encourage some guy that wants to be a welder or is more inclined toward the vo-tech type education? Could you expand on that? We'll start with you, Mr. Mullins.

Mr. MULLINS. Thank you, Senator. Absolutely, the products like the Smart Helmet are designed to create jobs, to empower workers with something we call "knowledge transfer." Very complex activities, very complex tasks can be broken down and shown visually so that they're much easier to comprehend, to understand. It allows workers to put on a device like the Smart Helmet and be able to perform a task or even work in a job that they don't have any prior experience with.

It's substantiated by independent studies. Elaborating on the Boeing and Iowa State study that I mentioned in my testimony, they used augmented reality to train workers that had never before put together aircraft wings. Those workers, using augmented reality, were able to put the wings together, although they had no experience doing it, in 30 percent less time and with over 90 percent less errors than with any other training method.

What was really fascinating, if you read the study in its entirety, is that the second time those workers used augmented reality to assemble the wings, the mean error rate was zero. They were able to remove human error from the equation completely, and these were workers that had never before performed those activities, never worked in those jobs.

You mentioned welding, specifically, in the question. We have seen in our own customer base augmented reality used to train welders faster than previously possible, far exceeding the rates at which a successful welder can be deployed than even that in dedicated trade schools for welding. I think the opportunity here is actually to not just create jobs, but to improve the concept of worker portability, where a worker who may have spent a substantial amount of time in their career in a job or even an entire segment of industry that may not be relevant anymore—to give them the opportunity, without having to take multiple years off to reskill and retrain, to enter the workforce in a very productive way in a dramatically shorter period of time.

I think that augmented reality has a huge opportunity to help us not just create new jobs, but to reshape the workforce, and to fill the jobs that we have a very difficult time filling today with the workers that wake up in the morning and want to make a living. They want to do something and don't have the experience today to do it.

Senator WICKER. In the minute and a half we have left, does anyone else want to take a stab at that?

Mr. Pierre-Louis?

Mr. PIERRE-LOUIS. Thank you, Senator Wicker. As you were speaking, I was thinking of a few things that came to mind. One is the fact that a career in video game design, of which there are three schools in the city that actually have video game design and there's a company there. People often leave that and go into many industries, because the skills you learn in learning how to make simulations are actually broader and have lots of applications, one of which is an exciting technology that one of our members, Microsoft, is working on now.

So they've developed a visor called "HoloLens," and it's a visor that's see-through but you can have data input into it. They're working with an educational publisher named *Pearson* to develop educational online tutorials, whether it's for nursing, construction, engineering, and so you're able to retrain—they are working on developing this program now on retraining people into various careers, and you're able to do that in a very consistent manner. Just as Mr. Mullins discussed, when you have consistent training, you can get to a place where all workers are learning the same craft in an even-paced way. So a lot of exciting technologies.

Senator WICKER. Mr. Blau?

Mr. BLAU. Thanks. It's a great question, and I just wanted to tell you that I have the great opportunity to talk to many businesses around the world, both in core business market and consumer as well. The inquiries that come to my desk are wide ranging, and in terms of creating jobs, we can see opportunities in the retail sector, in insurance, in training, in science and education, manufacturing, and I could go on and on about the list. So we really think that there's an opportunity for this technology to be put into businesses for a wide variety of use cases.

I liked your question, though, about how many different people could use the technology. We think it could be used from children all the way through adults and elders, too, and in businesses and the consumer domain, and not only in just the United States, but there are a lot of use cases we see in foreign countries. I have the great opportunity to travel to Asia and to Europe, and I get a lot of questions there about how to use the technology.

So we really think it can be broadly applicable, and we think it can create jobs, and not only that, but we think it's going to be beneficial to all of these industries that want to use it because it's going to improve productivity, maybe give a great entertainment experience, and that alone will create a lot of jobs in the future.

Senator WICKER. Well, thank you very much.

Mr. Chairman, if you'll indulge me for another second or two— Mr. Mullins, you thought enough of your alma mater to mention it in your opening statement. I'm on the Board at the Merchant

Marine Academy and very proud to be an active member of the Board. Are you a member of the Alumni Association?

Mr. MULLINS. Thank you for the question. I think that I will be in the near future. Thank you, Senator.

[Laughter.]

Senator WICKER. They could use you, and I would have to say—and I think you would agree—that the skills you learned as an engineering student have served you well in your chosen career.

Mr. MULLINS. Without a doubt. I think that the skills and the broad applicability of engineering across the Merchant Marine and all the factors involved definitely helped in how I conceptualized augmented reality being deployed in the workforce.

Senator WICKER. And that semester at sea made you a well-rounded person, don't you think?

Mr. MULLINS. Yes, sir. One of the best experiences of my life.

Senator WICKER. Great. Thank you so much.

Thank you, Mr. Chairman.

The CHAIRMAN. Senator Wicker, I was just waiting for the fund-raising pitch there.

[Laughter.]

The CHAIRMAN. Senator Peters?

STATEMENT OF HON. GARY PETERS, U.S. SENATOR FROM MICHIGAN

Senator PETERS. Thank you, Mr. Chairman.

Fascinating testimony here today, and I had the pleasure of seeing some of the applications before the hearing here, and I appreciate you bringing some of your applications for us to experience.

But, Mr. Hanke, I want to continue to go down the lines of your concerns about cybersecurity, something that I worry a great deal about. Being a member of the Commerce Committee here and also a member of the Homeland Security Committee, I believe that probably our most significant threat that we face is cyber threats to industry and to national security issues and, in particular, to small businesses.

Your business—you talked about as you launched the Pokémon GO the number of cyber attacks that you had repeatedly. I know you're a fairly small company of 75 employees, a startup, incredibly successful, but nevertheless not large enough to be dealing with all of the whack-a-mole that you deal with, as you mentioned in your testimony.

I actually have introduced bipartisan legislation called the Small Business Cyber Security Improvement Act, which we're hoping will create more collaboration with small businesses, the Department of Homeland Security, SBA, and other ways in which small businesses can learn some best practices, perhaps, or some things that they need to be aware of. But I'd be curious as to some of the lessons that you learned in dealing with those cyber attacks, something that might be helpful for us as we're thinking about how we assist other small businesses who have great ideas but are also potentially exposing not only themselves and their customers, but the wider net of potential cyber attacks.

Mr. HANKE. Well, I welcome the opportunity to raise awareness for that topic some more, so thank you for bringing it up. In terms of what lessons did we learn, the variety of attacks and the origin of those attacks is worldwide. It was eye-opening to really under- stand that those attacks are coming in from all quarters and the degree of really smart engineers out there in many places around the world that perhaps lack opportunity to pursue other things and devote themselves to these kinds of attacks and formulating them. The sophistication of these attacks is impressive, from a tech- nology point of view. It is not something I think a company that doesn't have experience and doesn't have substantial resources is going to be successful in fending off. So the idea of best practices and sharing that, I think, is a sound one. It takes resources to im- plement those. It costs money.

A good place to start might be with the cloud providers them- selves, Amazon and Google, you know. A lot of people host on those services, and I think they do a very good job. But that is kind of the first line of defense, and then beyond that, there are additional things that companies have to do at the corporate network level, as well as at the product level. So I'm afraid I don't have a magic solution for you, other than just at this point having an expanded appreciation for the degree and sophistication of what businesses are up against.

Senator PETERS. Well, I appreciate that. I appreciate that we don't have a magic wand, but that's something we obviously have to be thinking about every day.

Mr. PIERRE-LOUIS. Senator Peters, that's a great question. One of the things that companies are doing more and more now is building in cybersecurity and data security into the design of all the applications, and that's as necessary as having a lock on your door now, because we know it's a threat. It's been reported on, and it happens.

One of the helpful developments over the past few years has been the DOJ and FTC working together to provide some rules that allow for information sharing, for example, among and be- tween companies so that they can analyze threats and sometimes even work with law enforcement, and I guess I would encourage lawmakers to continue that encouragement and to continue that practice, because you learn a lot by collaboration, and knowing that you don't have the threat of litigation for doing so or an increased threat of other matters is helpful. So I guess I would encourage continued collaboration and encouraging that collaboration.

Senator PETERS. Thank you.

Yes?

Mr. CALO. Thank you, Senator Peters. One thing I would say— and this applies more broadly than augmented reality, certainly— is that it's not just the companies by themselves that are able to identify issues. It's also researchers. One of the problems that we as researchers face is that we worry that our reverse engineering or our attempts to figure out what the flaws might be with a device will be met with legal challenges, so, for example, if you're poking around in the software in the firmware that you're violating the Computer Fraud and Abuse Act, or perhaps you're violating the anti-circumvention provision of the Digital Millennium Copyright Act.

So I think the one thing that the government can do is to make it absolutely crystal clear to researchers that they're allowed to look into these products, like Internet of Things and augmented reality, to make sure that they are as safe as can be and to identify flaws. I think that would be very empowering to the research community to help with the cybersecurity effort.

Senator PETERS. Right. Thank you. I appreciate it. I'm out of time.

The CHAIRMAN. Thank you, Senator Peters.

Senator Daines, do you want a minute, or do you—I could ask some questions in the interim, but if you're ready, go ahead.

STATEMENT OF HON. STEVE DAINES, U.S. SENATOR FROM MONTANA

Senator DAINES. Thank you, Mr. Chairman. It's just-in-time manufacturing here.

[Laughter.]

Senator DAINES. Speaking of that, prior to my time in the Senate, I spent many years helping build software companies and so forth in remote places like Montana, believe it or not.

So for Mr. Pierre-Louis, can you talk about the job creation potential in the AR space, particularly in rural communities?

Mr. PIERRE-LOUIS. Sure. What we're seeing with augmented reality and what we're seeing with mixed reality is an ability to train from afar, communicate from afar, and to collaborate from afar, so there are lots of opportunities. I think about education, for example. Earlier, I talked about the fact that Microsoft was using HoloLens to create online tutorials for a number of jobs. Those that have been highlighted are nursing, construction, engineering. But in rural communities, you can also do a lot of training and a lot of repairs. So I think it allows for that collaboration while at the same time providing a consistency to that experience.

Senator DAINES. One thing we're seeing is what used to be a liability when I was kid growing up north of Yellowstone Park—we always thought it was an asset, but the rest of the world—it's funny—it's a tremendous quality of life asset, where you can have your cake and eat it, too, particularly for the digital natives. We can attract and retain truly world-class talent. They don't want to go anywhere else, because they don't have traffic jams, and they're 15 minutes away from world-class skiing and backpacking and so forth.

Speaking about the next generation, a question I have is you think of the AR-VR industry—it's expected to reach revenues, my understanding is, of $100 billion kind of numbers by the year 2025. What types of skills do you believe younger generations need to focus on to fill these new jobs created by this industry?

Mr. PIERRE-LOUIS. Well, there are a couple of different things that we've seen in our industry. First, in terms of our consumer base, we have a very digital, very active base, and they let us know what they think of everything from game plots to return policies. So you get a lot of feedback of what's important. One of the things that has become very important is opportunities not only to play the games, but to learn how to make the games. So that ability has led people to lots of other things. For example, there are 131 schools in California that have video game programs, and those game programs can lead you to jobs in aerospace, not just in games. So there are lots of opportunities to do that.

But what we're also seeing is because they want to get into game design, they're actually very interested in more STEM, and the more STEM you learn, the more you can play in this space, because we are becoming a very digital society and you need to understand from an early age, not just algebra, but how you put it all together. I think it is actually motivating lots of younger people, and it's actually having a spike in women and minorities wanting to get into these fields because it's much more exciting. It's almost a back-door way of getting people more into science, generally, because you come in on the game end, and you end up making simulations for airliners.

Senator DAINES. Yes. In the time I have left, I want to switch over to vehicle safety.

Mr. Mullins, thank you for the great demo. Montana has the second highest rate of vehicle ownership per capita in the Nation. We lost over 200 lives last year in Montana on the roads. We heard today that AR is one of the most powerful ways to improve safety on the road. I don't doubt that at all.

In rural areas, we drive on gravel roads. We drive in very unpredictable conditions. We have elk and deer, sometimes bison, crossing the roadways, and we have roads, in fact, that don't even register on GPS. A driver could be on the road for hours without seeing another car.

We have folks who come out to Montana from the cities. They're frightened when traveling with me in my pickup. They won't see another vehicle for many, many—you know, extended periods of time during the night, and I tell them, "We're safe. If we break down, there'll be a rancher that'll be here and be very kind. He'll take care of us."

So how can you explain—or could you explain how these safety benefits will translate to rural America where we have a disproportionate share of the automobile fatalities in our nation?

Mr. MULLINS. Senator, this is an excellent application for augmented reality in vehicles, both in newer vehicles and more and more with the option to easily upgrade with aftermarket products. Cars, through their automated driver systems and more and more automation—they have sensors. They have a wealth of information to understand some of the problems that you described. You know, elk in the road is not a funny issue, and it seems like something that we could very easily fix by tapping into the sensors that are in the vehicle that understand that there's an obstruction, there's something else there, and to be able to visually call to the attention of the driver in a way—in an amount of time that they can react to it and they can respond to it.

You know, it starts with something seemingly simple like that, saving a small number of lives and then expanding and looking at how those sensors that are designed for autonomous driving in urban environments could be adapted to take that same sense of awareness that the vehicle gets and adapting them specifically to the hazards of rural driving and the unique requirements there that could lead to saving lives.

Senator DAINES. Thank you.

It's amazing how fast 5 minutes goes by, Mr. Chairman, so thank you.

The CHAIRMAN. Thank you, Senator Daines. You asked a number of questions that I was going to ask, so I'd like to associate myself with the questions from the Senator from Montana.

And, Mr. Hanke, those roads that don't show up on most maps—does Google Earth and Google Maps capture those roads in Montana that Senator Daines drives down?

Mr. HANKE. Well, it sounds like there's some more work to do there. I will contact my colleagues at Google and let them know that there's room for improvement in their products.

Senator DAINES. Except for that road to my favorite elk hunting spot. I want to keep that private.

[Laughter.]

The CHAIRMAN. He doesn't want that to show up on any map.

Thank you, Senator Daines.

So, Senator Booker, have you played Pokémon GO?

Senator BOOKER. I refuse to answer that question on the grounds it might incriminate me.

[Laughter.]

The CHAIRMAN. Well, I was hoping that perhaps you could counsel Senator Nelson and I about how to do it someday, maybe walk us through it.

But, anyway, Senator Booker is probably one of the highest tech Senators we have on our Committee.

STATEMENT OF HON. CORY BOOKER, U.S. SENATOR FROM NEW JERSEY

Senator BOOKER. Mr. Chairman, you'll have to forgive me, because I literally have to dart out, but I didn't want to do so without just thanking everybody for being here and thanking you for your testimony.

Mr. Calo, I really appreciated your white paper about a lot of the legal issues and a lot of the other concerns. I'm really excited about this space. I don't think we even understand fully how it can be enhancing life, especially—there are a number of us who have gotten together on a bill around the Internet of Things—just the potential for health, well-being, safety, education, and learning. It's just such an extraordinarily exciting world.

This is a wonderful bipartisan space, because I've been very vocal on the Commerce Committee about how our regulations are choking a lot of innovations, and we need to make sure that we create a nurturing environment where we can continue to be the number one exporter of innovation here in America. You know, I joked in another hearing about how we had a regulatory framework for drones that was so choking and forcing drone innovation to go into other countries that, frankly, if that kind of regulation was around during the time of the Wright brothers, we would have never gotten the airline industry off the ground here.

So I'm very excited about it. But one question I wanted to ask before, literally, I sprint out for a meeting is that one of the other areas or the problem that we have as a result of this—and I really appreciate, Mr. Pierre-Louis, your comments about diversification and even a richer pipeline of diversity coming into STEM subjects. But I have this continuing concern about the fact that we do not have a level playing field in terms of access to the Internet right now, access to broadband, and what that could mean, especially as these new opportunities are coming.

In terms of a fair playing field, does anybody have any ideas about what we should be thinking about in terms of the government's obligation to try to make sure, as this superhighway is sort of taking people to these new worlds of innovation and opportunity, that folks are not being left behind? I didn't know if anybody would want to comment on that.

Mr. HANKE. I would love to comment on that. You know, as somebody who grew up in a rural area, in my case, west Texas— I'm headed back there to visit my family at the end of the week. I will arrive there, and I will not be able to use the products that I work on there, because I will be limited to 3G service when I arrive.

I do think it's an important issue, not only to access the products that people are bringing to market, but to inspire the youth there to know about these things, to be aware of them, to pursue careers in that area. Virtually all of our communications and much of our learning and access to information now is moving to mobile devices, and if one is sipping through a narrow straw in terms of the ability to consume information, to pursue opportunity there, that does feel like a very limiting factor to me.

I am certainly empathetic to the youth growing up in my hometown. I would like for them to discover and be inspired by opportunities that will lead them to a happy and prosperous future. A lot of those opportunities now are coming through that pipe. So if government can broaden it, that strikes me as a very good thing for the government to put its weight behind and to achieve.

Senator BOOKER. Mr. Chairman, with that, I'm going to say thank you. I just want to—again, having read the white paper that was about a lot of fears and concerns, I hope—when we have new innovations going on—that we don't allow a lot of our fears of the worst case scenario force us to over-regulate or do things that inhibit thinkers and imaginers and innovators from doing their work. That's one area I really do think there's a lot of bipartisan commitment to. So thank you very much, and forgive me for not being able to stay longer.

The CHAIRMAN. Thank you, Senator Booker, and not only on that issue, but also on the extension of broadband all over the country. There are a lot of places where I come from, too, that you can go to where you wouldn't be able to do the things that we're talking about here today.

Senator BOOKER. In New Jersey, we're very concerned about buffalo crossings as well.

[Laughter.]

The CHAIRMAN. Buffalo and elk and—yes.

Let me just ask a few questions here as we wrap up.

Mr. Mullins, one of the major impediments to the successful deployment of any technology is consumer adoption, and DAQRI's technology is largely designed for industrial applications. What barriers do you anticipate with regard to broader consumer adoption?

Mr. MULLINS. I think that's a great question. I think one of the largest barriers to transitioning to consumer adoption is actually the issue of the industry over-promising and under-delivering. The consumer expectation is very high, and there are the natural price sensitivities. When you roll out a technology to the enterprise first, the costs of the technology are measured by the return on investment and the value that is created in the enterprise.

I think we expect the augmented reality industry to follow the trends of the cellular telephone. Phones didn't start out as smartphones. They didn't even start out as the bricks we remember. They were first briefcases. They were very expensive and had limited coverage. But if they kept you connected and allowed you to make a decision, they were worth the investment, and that investment from enterprise created the infrastructure that ultimately led to consumers.

Technology moves a lot faster today, so I don't think it will take decades. But it will be slow, and I think that both regulations and the industry needs to do a good job of setting the expectation of consumers and fostering the development of augmented reality in the spaces that make a big impact today.

The CHAIRMAN. Mr. Blau, thoughts on the same subject, barriers to consumer adoption?

Mr. BLAU. Sure. Thank you for the question. It's a great question. The consumers, as Mr. Mullins said, are quite fickle and they have a high expectation of quality. And to be honest, augmented reality technology, as well as virtual reality, are not the same as what we see in video games today, for example, or special effects in movies, or even the quality of the apps that you have on your smartphone. You could say that the AR and VR—the quality of the experience is quite low today.

So one of the things that we ask you is to provide for an opportunity for innovation. Software developers, hardware developers must have the opportunity to create these exceptionally good experiences, and it won't be until then when we are able to put those technologies forward in the consumer market.

Not only that, but there has to be a clear price-to-value relationship. That's really critical, and that can't happen until the manufacturing is set up to be able to produce these devices at a mass market level. We're not talking tens of millions. We're talking hundreds of millions or billions of devices that need to get into market, and that is when we would think that the consumers would be ready for it. So the manufacturing is one.

Part of it has to do with the transparent display that you saw in the augmented reality headsets in the demonstrations. Those are relatively new inventions, and so those have to be developed over the next few years, and when they get good enough and, to be honest, to be like my glasses here, that's when consumers will think about adopting the headsets.

But also augmented reality may not come on a headset first. It may come in a smartphone or another form factor. So there are lots of different ways that augmented reality could come to consumers, for example, having a window which you can look through and see something on the other side that's augmented in a particular way, like an airplane window, for example, or even going to a store to try on clothes through something called a smart mirror. You stand in front of it, and it's an augmented reality experience that can show you different clothes and what they would look like rather than having to try them on. So those are some of the technologies that have to develop before it's really going to hit the consumer.

The CHAIRMAN. Mr. Pierre-Louis, last year, this committee held the first congressional hearing on the Internet of Things, and we heard input from industry on how lawmakers should or, in some cases, shouldn't legislate to foster innovation. Today, we're holding another first of its kind hearing on augmented reality, which I think is a very exciting and emerging technology with tremendous potential.

What can we as lawmakers do to help this technology flourish? Or maybe even more importantly, what should we not do so that we don't in any way hinder the innovation that's happening out there?

Mr. PIERRE-LOUIS. That's a terrific question. Let me tell you one of the things that our industry has done to meet market concerns, and that's a great template for how we develop our practices. In the sphere of providing information about games, we've got a rating system where we provide age appropriateness and some content descriptions to tell parents what's in the game. So not only is it E for everyone or T for teen, but what are the kinds of things you might see in there, and there's comic mischief, mild violence— they'll have different lists of things.

But when you get into the mobile environment, and people are moving around, you need different ways of allowing people to understand what's happening in the app world because some of those games are—and not just games, but other programs are getting rated as well, and so the industry created new descriptors on interactivity. So it tells you if you are sharing your location in a game or if you're on a chat function or if there's in-app purchasing.

So if you were to download the Pokémon GO app on the Google Play store, it'll tell you you're sharing your location, and there are in-app purchases. What it won't say is there's user chat, because there's no chat between users. It's really meant for people to play or parents to play with their kids. It's an individual game. That allows users to understand in a very simple way what they're getting, and that's an innovation that developed because consumers wanted to know more about it.

I think allowing that kind of development to occur makes the most sense, because it's meeting consumer demand. There's a lot of acceptance, and what we're seeing is 86 percent and higher of people not only aware but really appreciative of what we provide. And when the FTC comes and looks at the programs that we do, they laud them and say, "You're doing it the right way. You're the gold standard," both in terms of our ratings and also our privacy offerings. So I think allowing that kind of market dynamism to grow is the right approach, and then to report back what's going on so that regulators and policymakers see that the marketplace is working.

The CHAIRMAN. This technology, augmented reality, is on track to be a very disruptive technology in a number of different markets. Why has America been able to lead the effort, and how can America maintain its position as a leader in the field as AR technology becomes more prevalent? And I guess I would—Mr. Pierre-Louis, Mr. Blau—anybody on the panel that would like to respond to that question.

Mr. BLAU. Thanks again for the question. It's a great question. I just want to point out that it was the United States military that had a big part in the invention of the computers, per se. In the 1960s, there was a famous professor, Ivan Sutherland, that created the first head-mounted display at the University of Utah. In the 1980s, it was American inventors that brought forward virtual reality and pioneered computer graphics.

So these are innately American inventions, and I'm not saying that there are other parts of the world that haven't contributed. But through the great universities and the opportunity that we've had as Americans, there has been this concentration that's here. But part of the industry today is not in the United States. It's in Asia, and that's the manufacturing. So part of what these companies are producing—they can design them here, but they can't manufacture them here, not all of them.

So it's not an even playing field around the world. If we potentially could enable more businesses in the United States to make advanced technology in a way that is competitive globally, that would be a great help.

The CHAIRMAN. Mr. Calo?

Mr. CALO. I think that's a great question, Chairman. I just want to point out that with respect to one of the previous transfers of technology of our time, the Internet, the military, once again, was absolutely instrumental in creating the Internet, and, as well, the American universities were instrumental.

But one of the reasons why even today, the United States remains dominant in terms of the Internet is because in the mid 1990s, we wisely immunized platforms for what users do on those platforms in the form of Section 230 of the Communications Decency Act. That immunity allowed the platforms to be open and to flourish and to have all kinds of contribution. Getting that right first, I think, gave us an enormous competitive advantage.

Here, there may be analogs to make sure we understand where liability is distributed, to make sure that we have adequate privacy and security to the point that consumers feel comfortable, just as they had to once get comfortable with banking online. So I understand the need not to impede innovation through regulation. At the same time, sometimes we can clarify liability and privacy rules in ways that permit the technology to flourish.

Mr. HANKE. I'm glad you're raising that question. I do think that AR represents one of those big transitional moments in technology. You know, we saw the move from the mainframe computer and IBM, and sort of the mantle was inherited by Microsoft, and we saw companies like Apple step in and kind of inherit the mantle in mobile and Google in web services.

AR represents one of those transitions, and it means there will potentially be new industry leaders, new very large companies that emerge. In the past, those have been U.S. companies. This time, it's a jump ball. It's not guaranteed that the successors are going to be U.S. companies. We operate in a global economy. I don't think it necessarily should be our expectation that we just naturally inherit that. We're going to have to go compete for it. But what we can do is create an environment where the companies here do have an equal playing field in terms of competing to be those leaders in that next generation of technology.

Having clarity around issues such as privacy with our colleagues in Europe so that we actually understand what the requirements are for a U.S. company to operate in Europe—that's an area where there's some ambiguity at the moment—market access in countries in Asia where it is currently very difficult or impossible for U.S. companies to offer services—those are things that are impediments to the ability of American companies to compete in this important market.

Mr. PIERRE-LOUIS. I'll just also add real quickly that our markets really encourage innovation, and that innovation is allowed to sprout in all manner of places, and that's the beauty of these new technologies. So when we think about new technologies and tech spaces, we think of places like Silicon Valley; Redmond, Washington; Silicon Alley in New York.

But then you have a company like Magic Leap, which is one of our members, that's creating mixed reality technology. They're based in Fort Lauderdale, not a place where people really think about as a technology hub. But by having someone create an idea and others coalesce around it, they now have more than 800 employees here in the U.S., maybe up to 1,000 at this point, all around an idea of innovation. So you can create new hubs around this idea of innovation and market-driven forces. That's what's exciting about what we do here.

The CHAIRMAN. Well, we're waiting for a Silicon Prairie to strike in South Dakota. Any time you guys want to bring your companies out there, we welcome them. We've got a great business climate. The actual climate this time of the year can get a little cold.

Senator Blumenthal has arrived.

Senator Blumenthal?

STATEMENT OF HON. RICHARD BLUMENTHAL,
U.S. SENATOR FROM CONNECTICUT

Senator BLUMENTHAL. Thanks so much, Mr. Chairman. Thanks for having the hearing.

As many of you may know, the incidence of traffic crashes and deaths has increased. In fact, according to the National Highway Traffic Safety Administration, there were 17,775 traffic deaths within the first 6 months of 2016, which is an increase of 10 percent above 2015. And in 2014, the Department of Transportation found that over 3,000 people were killed and 430,000 injured in car crashes that involved distracted drivers.

An article from just yesterday's *New York Times* blames the new mobile apps, many of them employing augmented reality technologies, as major contributors to the rise in traffic deaths due to distracted driving. I'm not going to quote from the article. You may have seen it. But it indicates that, unfortunately, the misuse of such applications has already resulted in a lot of deadly disasters.

So my question is—beginning with Mr. Hanke—how has Niantic responded to this dramatic increase in distracting driving as a result of your products, most especially—well, some of the ones that have been mentioned here so far this morning?

Mr. HANKE. I'm very glad you raised that issue. As a parent, you know, I've got teenagers that are learning to drive, and just as somebody out on the highways, it's certainly an issue that I think is a big one and that we have to wrestle with and try to improve the current situation.

With regard to the *New York Times* article, I'll take this opportunity to correct the statement that they made about Pokémon GO players being able to play Pokémon GO while driving. We've actually adopted what I think is an industry-leading policy to disable operation of the application in terms of capturing Pokémon or accessing the Poké stops in the game when the person is moving above a speed that is reasonable for a person to walk or run. So that is the current state of the game, and that's what we've done to try to mitigate this.

At the same time, I think it is, to some degree, an issue of personal responsibility. There are other contributors to distracted driving as well. In one of the studies I read recently was that consumption of food in the car was actually one of the leading causes of traffic accidents. But I do think it's an important problem, and we've taken it upon ourselves to proactively limit the use of our application in that situation.

Senator BLUMENTHAL. Why is not the use of Pokémon GO unsafe at any speed?

Mr. HANKE. Well, it is safe when you're walking. Many people like to walk and jog to use the application. It's an activity that we encourage.

Senator BLUMENTHAL. But if you're driving at any speed, isn't it unsafe?

Mr. HANKE. It is a question of what we can detect and control within the application. We do not have a mechanism to detect when somebody is driving, per se. We have the ability to detect their speed of movement. Whether they're a driver, a passenger, a bike rider, a runner or walker, we don't have a definitive way of understanding that. So since we don't have perfect information, we use speed as the——

Senator BLUMENTHAL. So you're saying that the app doesn't detect what the activity is that causes the speed.

Mr. HANKE. That's correct, yes.

Senator BLUMENTHAL. Why isn't that possible, and why shouldn't you then just say anybody who's moving is putting themselves or somebody else at risk? And that, until we figure out a way to detect the difference between somebody walking, jogging, driving, any speed will, in effect, deactivate this program? My feeling is someone distracted by this kind of activity is unsafe at any speed.

Mr. HANKE. Well, we've taken a position which, again, I think is—I'm not aware of any other applications in the industry that are doing what we're doing, which is stopping the use of the application above a speed that a human could move walking or running. In terms of going even further and eliminating the use of the application at any speed whatsoever that would inhibit somebody from using it while they're walking or jogging, personally, that feels like a step too far to me in terms of limitation on the ability to use such an application.

Senator BLUMENTHAL. Well, my time has expired. This has been a very useful and informative session. Again, I thank the Chairman for holding it. There are a lot of other questions that I have. I'll submit them in writing and look forward to your responses, and thank you for being here today.

The CHAIRMAN. Thank you, Senator Blumenthal.

I also want to echo what the Senator from Connecticut just said, and that is that we do appreciate you all being here and for sharing your insights about this. This is a really exciting field with lots of moving parts, many of which have been addressed today, and you've heard some of the concerns expressed as well. But we want to be in a position where we're enhancing the advancement of these technologies and innovation, not getting in the way of it, obviously interested in all the safety issues and privacy issues that are associated with any discussion of this subject.

But thank you for the light that you've shed on it today, and we'll look forward to continuing the dialog and discussion.

Senator Blumenthal has additional questions. Perhaps other members do as well. We'll ask them to submit them. We'll keep the record open for 2 weeks, and during that time, we're asking that Senators submit any questions for the record and that the witnesses as they receive them, as soon as they can, submit those answers back to the Committee.

So with that, thank you again, and this hearing is adjourned.

[Whereupon, at 4:28 p.m., the hearing was adjourned.]

APPENDIX

RESPONSE TO WRITTEN QUESTIONS SUBMITTED BY HON. MARCO RUBIO TO BRIAN BLAU

Question 1. As we conduct our oversight role as lawmakers, how can we ensure that technology start-ups, like Magic Leap, are able to continue to advance in the 21st century economy without imposing unnecessary red tape?

Answer. Red tape exists in many forms, and for augmented reality technology there are 4 areas that stand out as important when considering adding more or re moving red tape: (1) purchasing and accessing technology components, and then selling technology products in the global market, (2) hiring qualified workers, (3) protecting intellectually property, (4) technology certifications. Each of these areas have established laws, rules, and oversight organizations that often times pose obstacles in how a business wants to create technology and products. My comments here are not meant as a debate about the usefulness of red tape situations, but the one important point to be raised about augmented reality is that despite the hype and media attention it's a very new technology that needs time, lots of time, to mature. Red tape during this critical phase of development for augmented reality will only cause its growth to be held back.

During the next 5–10 years it's imperative that companies, like Magic Leap, have the resources necessary to develop and innovate as needed and operate unrestricted. Pre-guessing the level of augmented realities capabilities in the future to make new laws today, for whatever reason, should be carefully considered as these companies don't yet know fully how their future products will bring value to their customers. I do urge you to monitor, for example, how augmented reality would impact topics like privacy and security, but it's still too early to determine any new laws will be needed.

Question 2. In your opinion, would current regulations placed on the gaming and computer industry be appropriate to apply to this new generation technology?

Answer. Yes, in general, the existing laws on video games and overall computer technology are sufficient today to allow for the invention, innovation, product development and sale of augmented reality technology. Evidence is the proliferation of American technology globally, and our standing in the global technology market provides a great example of how a government can effectively help businesses flourish. That said, some issues, like repatriation of offshore funds and the ability to compete globally should be monitored and law subsequently adjusted as optimizing these programs could benefit U.S. companies in the future.

The most valuable way to help augmented reality businesses to profit is to promote the value of its technology across the spectrum of business operations. Help a business innovate and invent by not adding restrictions that hold back any type of early research, development, or deployment of products in this area.

Question 3. Autism is an issue I feel very passionate about and have worked on going back to my time in the Florida legislature. Some have suggested that augmented reality games can benefit people on the autism spectrum in terms of getting them out of the house and developing their social skills. Is the industry doing any of its own scientific research to determine the actual benefits of augmented gaming to people on the autism spectrum?

Answer. I'm positive that augmented reality technology can help those impacted by autism as its been helpful in many areas of medical and health fields. Typically, a technology company tends to focus on general use cases, and that is what we are seeing with most augmented reality technology providers today. Unfortunately, the answer the Senators question means that there isn't an industry initiative on autism, at least to any large degree. What we do see efforts from the medical profession in how augmented reality can impact research, diagnosis and treatment of autism. It's appropriate that any advancement come from the medical industry given the unique requirements for any technology use in healthcare.

That said, I can imagine (without being a trained medical professional) that augmented reality can indeed help in many situations with regard to autism. Augmented reality can be used in social situations to bring together people who are not physically in the same place. It can be used in "training", and for autism I can imagine this means therapy using techniques like video games and interactive media content to stimulate thinking and reasoning. Augmented reality will be a great tool for training in scenarios that need to be practiced and repeated, or even providing simulations of real situations to help prepare those with autism for all types of daily life.

Question 4. What would you say our high schools and universities can be doing better in the coming years to ensure that people in Florida and in the United States acquire the skills and preparation to fill these jobs?

Answer. The best way to prepare for developing augmented reality technology, and what I would tell my own family and children, is to be educated. An agenda of learning in science and technology as well as business are important base layers for anyone who wants to be part of a technology development company. My own experience also mirrors that line of thought. I was fortunate to grow up in Orlando Florida where I attended Lake Brantley High School in Altamonte Springs, and then I received a Bachelor and Masters degrees, both in Computer Science from the University of Central Florida. In all three I was given and then took the opportunity to advance my interests in technology and it's as important as any to support these institutions in the same way they supported me.

Preparing to use augmented reality, vs making the technology, is easier. If made well and if designed for optimal use cases, augmented reality technology will be easy to master as it's designed with the person in mind. Typically, the user interface in augmented reality applications is natural and supports human gestures and voice. If done well I would expect augmented reality to be more easily adopted than even basic PC computers, which required detailed knowledge of a keyboard, mouse, and intricate on-screen movements and manipulations. For augmented reality the driving use case is the person and their body movements, so any training should be focused in the more general use of computing in the workplace.

Question 5. What message would you like to send to educators and students alike about the industry's future and the opportunities it presents?

Answer. My message to educators and students on is simple: use and develop augmented reality (and its close cousin virtual reality) as it represents one of the most important next generation technologies that you will need to understand and use over the coming decades.

This means, focus on science, technology, math and business as a way to prepare institutions and individuals as they prepare to be part of the next wave of computing. Augmented reality and virtual reality are hyper-personal technologies, ones that we have and wear close to our bodies and ones that have the ability to mesh with the human perceptual system in ways that have never been available. This means future technologists will need to better understand the human condition and how it reacts to an environment filled with sensors and screens.

Question 6. The interface created by these new technologies can be a tremendous asset to the Department of Defense, especially for training. How can the Department of Defense collaborate with innovators to push the limits of mixed reality technologies to ensure our men and women in uniform continue to be the best trained and equipped fighting force on this Earth?

Answer. In drawing from my own experience attending, and then working as a research scientist at the University of Central Florida on virtual reality technologies, I observed one of the best methods for providing the crossover between military and education.

In Orlando, at least in the 1980s and 1990s, there was an explicit program to transfer core computer technology out of secret military programs into the public domain. I was a beneficiary of that program at UCF and its Institute for Simulation and Training that the U.S. Navy and Army funded. This program in part was based on use of military equipment, access to military contractors, direct funding of virtual realty projects, and promotion of what was developed into the education and science community. As we look back, that technology transfer was is now seen a basis for how we all now have advanced real time computer graphics today.

I fully encourage future programs that marry the ability of the U.S. military with advanced educational needs as it's a proven method, and in fact is one of the reasons that I'm providing these answers to you today.

RESPONSE TO WRITTEN QUESTION SUBMITTED BY HON. JOE MANCHIN TO
BRIAN BLAU

Question. As a former Governor and in my role as a United States Senator, I have remained committed to enhancing the job climate in my state so that West Virginians have good paying jobs and the skills to compete in the global economy. Part of this job growth is going to come from the technology sector. We are beginning to see an uptick in technology startups in different parts of the state, but I believe there are opportunities for tools such as augmented reality to enhance workforce training.

The technological advancements of the 21st century should not leave rural communities behind, and as West Virginia continues to develop its technology sector and train its workforce: How can augmented reality be used to train workers in the digital economy?

Answer. This is a great question and one that hopefully can help shed light on how augmented reality technology can be used to effectively train people in workplace tasks and skills. The core of the benefit of augmented reality is its unique approach to delivering information by using sophisticated graphics seen through head-mounted display (HMD) devices. These devices have the capability to let the user see sophisticated computer graphics, they type we are familiar with from video games and movies, superimposed over top of real world objects. Its this overlay capability that is augmented realities best feature and is the one that is at the core benefit of how it can be used in workplace training situations.

Imagine a worker who needs to be trained on various types of equipment. That training today can consist of reading manuals, watching videos, practicing on mockups, or on-the-job training using real equipment. But in many cases using the actual equipment, mockups, or even the videos are simply not available or sufficient enough to effectively train the employee, especially if the tasks require their hands to be busy. Augmented reality can help here as when using the HMD it can simulate the equipment, show it as matching overlays, and can train the worker over many types of situations and scenarios. The combination of graphics, step-wise instructions, performance analytics, and customizability means augmented reality will be a prime resource for many businesses who want to use effective training technology.

As stated in my prepared testimony the augmented reality market is really just getting started in 2016, and within 5 years will we will an increasing number of devices come to market. The real benefit, and to the point of the Senator's question, is how can the technology not only be used for training, but also in the remote locations that are prevalent in West Virginia but in many parts of the country. Augmented reality is an inherently mobile technology and many of the device and system providers have features that let these devices be operated anywhere. Even in this early stage in the market development of augmented reality some devices are being made robust for environments outside of the normal business office or manufacturing facility. This mobile capability is an important one as it means augmented reality can be used in a wide variety of locations, possibly even ones that don't support wireless communications.

In addition to being mobile, augmented reality will be a great communication device, bringing people together that are physically located in different places. Sometimes called "telepresence", many future augmented reality applications will bring people together by using audio, video, and combined with computer graphics will enhance workers ability to interact with each other and work together even though they are not in the same location. One great example is a field service technician who's job will be to monitor and repair machines and equipment at distant locations. A future worker, wearing augmented reality smartglasses, will have technology to let them directly connect to other employees at the home office. Not only can the augmented reality smartglasses provide instructions and guidance that were traditionally delivered in a paper manual or on a flat screen device like a tablet, but when connected to others the work can be accomplished cooperatively. The technician at the home office can see, via live video, exactly what the remote technician is seeing and can even enhance the graphics for the remote technician by drawing on their virtual field of view, sending additional information via the overlap capability, or providing voice feedback.

The final point to note is that the training scenarios for augmented reality are limitless, and as its so early in the development of the technology I both urge you and your constituents to investigate, learn and invest in augmented reality technology, but to do it in a way that allows for and leverages its growth and maturity. Investing in augmented reality technology today means gaining knowledge and experience and as the devices and systems advance over the next decade.

RESPONSE TO WRITTEN QUESTIONS SUBMITTED BY HON. MARCO RUBIO TO
RYAN CALO

Question 1. As we conduct our oversight role as lawmakers, how can we ensure
that technology start-ups, like Magic Leap, are able to continue to advance in the
21st century economy without imposing unnecessary red tape?

Answer. I am aware of no augmented reality specific regulations and do not anticipate any in the near feature. Indeed, I believe regulating AR at this early stage
would be unwise. That said, well thought out government interventions can sometimes help foster technological innovation.

For example, the early decision of Congress to immunize online platforms such
as Facebook for almost anything users do or say on the social network reduced the
threat of litigation and preserved the incentives for Facebook to keep its platform
relatively open and free. In my article *Open Robotics,* I discuss the potential need
to immunize hardware providers such as Magic Leap as well insofar as they open
up their platforms to third party innovation.[1]

Privacy and other consumer protection laws are critical in that they help reassure
consumers that new products and services are safe enough to try. Flexible intellectual property regimes help remove the shadow of litigation from new startups and
allow for the sharing of intellectual resources. Many argue that net neutrality rules
preserve the ability of new entrants into information service markets by prohibiting
incumbents from blocking or slowing down competing applications on their networks.[2] And of course the Federal Government is in a position to preempt state
laws, which can sometimes create a patchwork of regulation that makes it difficult
for companies to operate. Other ways the Federal Government can help companies
such as Magic Leap include procuring their products and investing in AR basic research.

Question 2. In your opinion, would current regulations placed on the gaming and
computer industry be appropriate to apply to this new generation technology?

Answer. My understanding is that most of the issues in gaming law deal with intellectual property, rights of publicity, and free speech. In addition, the gaming industry has set its own standards around safety, violence, privacy, and gaming addic-
tion. I see all of these issues applying with equal or perhaps greater force to augmented reality. AR is a product and it needs to be safe for its intended use. Content
within AR is subject to copyright but also fair use and other exceptions that protect
consumers and innovators. And, importantly, AR should enjoy full constitutional
protection under the First Amendment as does content on the Internet and games
in other formats.[3]

Question 3. Autism is an issue I feel very passionate about and have worked on
going back to my time in the Florida legislature. Some have suggested that augmented reality games can benefit people on the autism spectrum in terms of getting
them out of the house and developing their social skills. Is the industry doing any
of its own scientific research to determine the actual benefits of augmented gaming
to people on the autism spectrum?

Answer. Thank you for your important work on autism. The Tech Policy Lab at
the University of Washington is committed to inclusive tech policy. The augmented
reality whitepaper I submitted to the record discusses the potential for AR to help
people with disabilities. We consulted with disability experts in the course of our
research and they told us that AR has enormous potential to help individuals with
physical and cognitive disabilities.

We did not engage with the autism research community superficially but I am
aware of considerable research into the ways AR could be used to help autistic children. For example, the Autism Glass project at Stanford University uses AR to help
autistic children better recognize emotional states in others.[4] Recent research out
of Cambridge University leverages AR to help draw autistic children into pretend
play.[5] There is also an extensive literature suggesting that robotics can help clinical
scientists study and address autism for similar reasons as AR.[6]

Question 4. What would you say our high schools and universities can be doing
better in the coming years to ensure that people in Florida and in the United States
acquire the skills and preparation to fill these jobs?

[1] See *https://papers.ssrn.com/sol3/papers.cfm?abstract ▌id=1706293.*
[2] E.g., *https://papers.ssrn.com/sol3/papers.cfm?abstract ▌id=1684677.*
[3] See *Reno* v. *American Civil Liberties Union,* 521 U.S. 844 (1997); *Brown* v. *Entertainment Merchants Association,* 564 U.S. 786 (2011).
[4] Visit *http://autismglass.stanford.edu/.*
[5] See *http://ieeexplore.ieee.org/document/7000596/.*
[6] See *https://www.ncbi.nlm.nih.gov/pmc/articles/PMC3223958/* (collecting studies).

Answer. A wide array of skills is needed to work in emerging industries such as augmented reality. These include so-called STEM skills, but also creative design, entrepreneurship, and the humanities. After all, someone has to dream up the narratives, the characters, the landscapes, the device design, the user interface, and the other aspects of AR that make it a worthwhile and wondrous experience. It is also increasingly clear that high schools and especially universities should be thinking of ways to break down barriers between disciplines and create opportunities for interdisciplinary collaboration. At the University of Washington Tech Policy Lab, one of our goals is to produce students comfortable speaking across disciplines. We do so in part by placing students into interdisciplinary teams like the team of computer scientists, information scientists, and lawyers that worked on the AR whitepaper I submitted as my written testimony.

Question 5. What message would you like to send to educators and students alike about the industry's future and the opportunities it presents?

Answer. I agree with my fellow panelists that augmented reality is already an exciting industry and will only grow, generating many opportunities for students with the right set of skills.

Question 6. The interface created by these new technologies can be a tremendous asset to the Department of Defense, especially for training. How can the Department of Defense collaborate with innovators to push the limits of mixed reality technologies to ensure our men and women in uniform continue to be the best trained and equipped fighting force on this Earth?

Answer. The Department of Defense has a long track record of fostering new technologies that ultimate become engines of American innovation. Augmented reality is one example; robotics and the Internet are two others. My hope is that the DOD can continue to fund basic research into new technologies to help keep the United States in a leadership position globally. Moreover, DOD should remain in dialogue with other sectors—such as athletics, medicine, and even the prison system—who may use AR for training purposes so that the knowledge that is produced in one sector can be shared efficiently across civilian and military contexts.

An important component of both civilian and military use of AR is ensuring adequate security. Obviously insecure AR can be physically dangerous to the user. I am aware of several ongoing around AR security and would be happy to connect your office to relevant researchers if useful.[7]

RESPONSE TO WRITTEN QUESTION SUBMITTED BY HON. JOE MANCHIN TO RYAN CALO

Question. As a former Governor and in my role as a United States Senator, I have remained committed to enhancing the job climate in my state so that West Virginians have good paying jobs and the skills to compete in the global economy. Part of this job growth is going to come from the technology sector. We are beginning to see an uptick in technology startups in different parts of the state, but I believe there are opportunities for tools such as augmented reality to enhance workforce training.

The technological advancements of the 21st century should not leave rural communities behind, and as West Virginia continues to develop its technology sector and train its workforce: How can augmented reality be used to train workers in the digital economy?

Answer. Augmented reality and virtual reality enhance workforce training by making it easier to teach new skills but also by providing a variety of training environments on a single platform. The availability of one AR headset could in theory dispense with the need for multiple, expensive facilities that may be difficult to maintain in rural communities. Thus, an individual could learn how to repair a robot or how to assist in a biology experiment using the same device and without the need for a mock repair shop or laboratory. For more examples—including how AR and VR could help retrain displaced or incarcerated workers more efficiently—please see the Tech Policy Lab whitepaper I submitted in connection to my testimony.

---

[7] See, *e.g., http://ar-sec.cs.washington.edu/research.html.*

RESPONSE TO WRITTEN QUESTIONS SUBMITTED BY HON. MARCO RUBIO TO JOHN HANKE

Question 1. As we conduct our oversight role as lawmakers, how can we ensure that technology start-ups, like Magic Leap, are able to continue to advance in the 21st century economy without imposing unnecessary red tape?

Answer. There may have been a time when start-ups in the technology sector could get off the ground and scale without having to be concerned about the policy and regulatory landscape, but I don't think that applies today. In developing both Ingress and Pokémon GO, we had to be sensitive to and be compliant with a host of laws and regulations, including those regarding data privacy, most notably the Children's Online Privacy Protection Act. Our attention to data privacy compliance at the early stage of the game's development proved to be so critically important because that was the central issue of concern from policymakers not long after Pokémon GO's launch.

While we certainly understand the concerns about the impact of regulations on start-up formation and success, there are areas where greater enforcement of existing regulations and increased attention to cybersecurity could be very useful to a start-up's success. We currently face challenges with respect to Pokémon GO, for example, with the creation of botnets and other methods that help players advance through the game. These services, which violate the integrity of our game and threaten the value of our intellectual property, are offered on the open market. We have been subject to near-constant hacking threats and attempts, to get access to our intellectual property and to our user data. The legal mechanisms to combat this kind of activity are costly and could be a barrier to a start-up's long term success.

Question 2. In your opinion, would current regulations placed on the gaming and computer industry be appropriate to apply to this new generation technology?

Answer. We do not support efforts to regulate the entertainment software industry based on its content. Entertainment software should be given the same First Amendment protections given other content-based industries, such as books, music, movies, and television programs. That said, we do support the work done by the Entertainment Software Ratings Board in providing age-based ratings and content descriptions, which together help consumers, particularly parents, make informed choices about the content they and their children see.

Question 3. Autism is an issue I feel very passionate about and have worked on going back to my time in the Florida legislature. Some have suggested that augmented reality games can benefit people on the autism spectrum in terms of getting them out of the house and developing their social skills. Is the industry doing any of its own scientific research to determine the actual benefits of augmented gaming to people on the autism spectrum?

Answer. It has been extremely gratifying to hear from our users and through press reports that Pokémon GO was played by and was helpful to many people on the autism spectrum. We are not aware of any industry-wide supported research on augmented reality and autism at this time, but we are aware of a number of research projects that have shown some promise in the use of augmented reality to help those on the autism spectrum better use and develop their social skills. For example, a team at Stanford University has developed and embedded artificial intelligence in Google Glass that enables someone with autism spectrum disorder to read and understand facial expressions and emotions of those around them. We welcome this kind of path-breaking research and are hopeful for more advances as the technology advances.

Question 4. What would you say our high schools and universities can be doing better in the coming years to ensure that people in Florida and in the United States acquire the skills and preparation to fill these jobs?

Answer. The work we are doing at Niantic, much like in other companies in the information technology industry, reinforce the value and importance of education in the so-called STEM fields—science, technology, engineering and mathematics. We are very much at the early stages of grasping the potential of augmented reality as not just an entertainment medium, but as a critical tool that can be of value to so many sectors of our economy.

Question 5. What message would you like to send to educators and students alike about the industry's future and the opportunities it presents?

Answer. We're very excited about the future of augmented reality and look forward to seeing its application in the future in areas that we did not anticipate today. One area that is certain to be impacted by the development of augmented reality is education and training. Augmented reality makes it possible to learn through experience, and in context, and that kind of learning has so much potential in fields ranging from medicine to construction. But even more fundamental is the potential for augmented reality to enhance learning and exploration by children at a young age, and not just in the classroom.

Question 6. The interface created by these new technologies can be a tremendous asset to the Department of Defense, especially for training. How can the Department of Defense collaborate with innovators to push the limits of mixed reality technologies to ensure our men and women in uniform continue to be the best trained and equipped fighting force on this Earth?

Answer. Military training is very much focused on building a foundation of experiences, and is centered on simulations that attempt to recreate various realities, whether that reality is in a fighter jet or a combat situation. Augmented reality certainly has the potential to enhance and grow the types of simulated environments that are used to train our military personnel.

Question 7. With the development of augmented reality (AR), we are allowing these new devices to see our private worlds. Many of these technologies transfer and/or retain data to ensure there is a seamless user experience. As you are well aware, this new technology opens up vulnerabilities which a malicious attacker could take advantage of data.

A Can you speak to how Niantic worked to mitigate data hacking on the Pokémon GO app?

Answer. Since the app was launched, Pokémon GO has been a target of numerous hacking efforts, including distributed denial of service attacks, unlawful data collection, or monetization through the use of botnets and other devices to help users gain advantages within the game.

For example, a backdoored version of the game was found on a file repository service not long after the game was launched. Attackers also sought to lure potential Pokémon users to malicious online sites that mimicked our own site, claiming users would be given additional features if they referred friends to the site, which led to more spamming. We've also seen strains of ransomware masquerading as a Pokémon GO app.

In these cases, as in others, working internally and with third parties, we've been able to take some of these malicious sites and apps down, but these challenges raise important questions about what technical and legal resources we have to combat efforts to misuse our intellectual property and target our users' data. It underscores the need for congressional review of existing laws relating to this area, including the Computer Fraud and Abuse Act and the Digital Millennium Copyright Act.

With respect to protecting our networks and data repositories, we utilize a number of applications and protocols that together represent best practices for our industry. We would be happy to provide additional details of these practices offline.

B Is the cybersecurity standard found on these systems a threat today? How can the data on this app, and others, be protected from malicious attacks and abuse without impeding the function of the system?

Answer. One of the most important cybersecurity practices is vigilance in protecting our networks. Today's cybersecurity best practice is likely tomorrow's vulnerability. For that reason, we not only monitor closely the integrity of our networks and systems, but we remain conscious of general threats that impact other data-intensive companies like ours. We would be happy to provide additional details of these practices offline.

Question 8. Earlier this year, there were reports of people chasing Pokémon Go characters in places like the Holocaust Memorial Museum and Arlington National Cemetery. What internal controls and self-policing is the industry undertaking to ensure that the solemn and sacred nature of places like these are respected?

Answer. It's worth sharing briefly how we decided the locations of Pokéstops and Gyms, which go back to the origins of Niantic Labs. First, the historical markers you can find on our first app, Field Trip, became one of the data sets we used to locate PokéStops and Gyms. Second, looking at Ingress, we thought about how to expand this set of interesting places that are public, visually recognizable, and safe places for people to visit. So we asked Ingress players to submit their ideas for local landmarks they thought were great places for people to visit, such as the Children's Museum in Brookings, South Dakota, or the ArtsPark at Young Circle in Hollywood Florida. Millions of places were contributed, and a subset of those contributions were included in Pokémon GO.

We recognize that many public places of historic significance may not be seen within the community they are located as suitable sites for Pokéstops and Gyms, and for that reason, we have an online form on our website that enables concerned citizens or administrators to request removal of Pokéstops and Gyms from specific locations.

RESPONSE TO WRITTEN QUESTION SUBMITTED BY HON. JOE MANCHIN TO
JOHN HANKE

Question. As a former Governor and in my role as a United States Senator, I have
remained committed to enhancing the job climate in my state so that West Virginians have good paying jobs and the skills to compete in the global economy. Part
of this job growth is going to come from the technology sector. We are beginning
to see an uptick in technology startups in different parts of the state, but I believe
there are opportunities for tools such as augmented reality to enhance workforce
training.

The technological advancements of the 21st century should not leave rural communities behind, and as West Virginia continues to develop its technology sector
and train its workforce: How can augmented reality be used to train workers in the
digital economy?

Answer. Augmented reality is designed to enhance people's daily life experiences
and help make the things that people do as human beings easier, safer, and in the
case of Pokémon Go, more fun. The technologies that allow Pikachu to roam our
neighborhoods by superimposing characters on mobile devices also have the potential to, among other things, improve the quality of health care by providing experi-
ence-driven training for doctors and nurses regardless of where they're located.
Similarly, AR can provide simulations that would enable construction workers or
miners to learn how best to respond to potential workplace hazards, which will provide a cost-effective tool to improve workplace safety.

RESPONSE TO WRITTEN QUESTIONS SUBMITTED BY HON. JOHN THUNE TO
BRIAN MULLINS

Question 1. In what ways will AR technology improve the productivity and safety
of the American worker and increase the competitiveness of the American workforce?

Answer. Given the broad interest in this topic across this senate committee, we
have prepared the following discussion on how Augmented Reality (AR) improves
the productivity, safety, and competitiveness of the workforce and enhances the
overall job climate in both industrialized and rural areas. AR empowers workers to
keep up with the increasing pace of technological change by providing an easy and
intuitive interface that fast-tracks the learning process. AR also makes workers
safer a variety of ways, including improving error rates and reducing cognitive load
which have a direct correlation to safety on the job.

I. Augmented Reality-based workforce training will prepare workers, across age groups and level of formal education, to compete and win in the global economy

Augmented Reality (AR) is a game-changer for job training and on-the-job skill
acquisition. Three decades of research supports the conclusion that AR improves
learning, productivity, accuracy, efficiency, and job satisfaction in a variety of contexts including manufacturing,[1,2] defense,[3] aerospace,[4] construction,[5] medicine[6] and
other sectors.

AR technology empowers experts and novices alike to quickly learn new skills or
be trained in a new area or sector—a particularly important benefit for workers who
have lost their jobs and cannot easily find work in their current industry. For example, AR-based workforce training can assist a laid-off coal miner who went directly
from high school into his or her career to be rapidly retrained in other, even unrelated, sectors without requiring two or four years of higher education. This in-

---

[1] Hou, Lei, *et al.,* "Using animated augmented reality to cognitively guide assembly." *Journal
of Computing in Civil Engineering* 27.5 (2013): 439–451.

[2] F. Loch, F. Quint and I. Brishtel, "Comparing Video and Augmented Reality Assistance in
Manual Assembly," *2016 12th International Conference on Intelligent Environments (IE),* London, 2016, pp. 147–150.

[3] Henderson, S. J.; Feiner, S. 2009. "Evaluating the benefits of augmented reality for task localization in maintenance of an armored personnel carrier turret." International Symposium on
Mixed and Augmented Reality, 2009 (ISMAR 2009). pp 135–144. Orlando, Florida.

[4] Caudell, T. P. and Mizell, D. W. 1992, Augmented reality: An application of heads-up display
technology to manual manufacturing processes. Proc. Ieee Hawaii International Conf. on Systems Sciences, 1992.

[5] Webster, Anthony, *et al.,* "Augmented reality in architectural construction, inspection and
renovation." *Proc. ASCE Third Congress on Computing in Civil Engineering.* 1996.

[6] K. Abhari *et al.,* "Training for Planning Tumour Resection: Augmented Reality and Human
Factors," in *IEEE Transactions on Biomedical Engineering,* vol. 62, no. 6, pp. 1466–1477, June
2015.

creased efficiency means that job training (or re-training) is no longer cost-prohibitive, especially for older or less formally-educated workers. This is critically important in states like West Virginia where workers have struggled to transition their skillsets into other fields in the midst of a decline in traditional sectors such as mining and manufacturing.

As referenced in our written testimony to this committee on November 16, 2016, Augmented Reality (AR) work instructions have been shown to improve accuracy, speed, focus and worker satisfaction when utilized in the training and operation of complex manufacturing tasks through visual, step-by-step work instructions overlaid directly on top of components to be assembled.[7] In addition to shorter task completion times and less assembly errors, the visual and spatial nature of AR enables a lower total task load and a reduction in the learning curve of novice assemblers, while increasing task performance relevant to working memory.[8] Compared with video-based work instructions, AR produces a significantly reduced number of errors and scores better in terms of time and overall mental workload.[9]

Today, the majority of learning experiences occur out of context. Classroom training, online training modules, and online synchronous training are all variations of didactic content presentation. Augmented reality will provide learning professionals opportunities to engage students and trainees with scalable and effective mechanisms to practice new skills in a hands-on manner, while still being supported by digital tools. This is especially valuable for workers who may not have seen a college or vocational classroom in more than twenty years, if at all.

How does AR improve the speed of knowledge-transfer and improve its retention? A key element is AR's ability to combine the real-world environment with digital information. When it comes to learning new concepts and skills, no training method beats hands-on experience. Experiencing the consequences of success and failure in real time helps us make neural connections that are much stronger and longer lasting than simply consuming content. Wearable head-up displays with AR capabilities give the wearer a view that fuses the complexity and messiness of the real world with the precision and reliability of a digital display, providing access to the real-world scene for the hands-on aspect of training, while enhancing it with didactic or reference information to keep us on track. It is notably effective in enhancing spatial reasoning.

II. Enhancing the overall job climate

At a macroeconomic level, Augmented Reality can enhance the job climate by increasing productivity, which increases demand, which then increases employment. For example, Augmented Reality is likely to increase demand for manufacturing jobs due to its ability to directly improve manufacturing productivity. Studies show that Augmented Reality technology delivers significant improvements in worker productivity in the context of manufacturing and assembly.[10] This higher growth in manufacturing productivity, however, does not lead to a decline in employment. According to empirical research conducted by Yale Economics Professor William Nordhaus, the evidence shows that "rapid productivity growth leads to increased rather than decreased employment in manufacturing," as increased productivity leads to lower prices, thereby expanding demand, which results in increased employment.[11]

III. Augmented reality applications for rural areas

Of course, even if increased demand for manufactured goods results in increased manufacturing employment, those jobs may be unavailable in some areas, especially in rural states, if there are few or no factories located there. But far from leaving rural communities behind, some of the strongest use cases for Augmented Reality (AR) are specifically tailored to rural industries. As several senators have an interest in this topic, we have prepared the following discussion on AR applications in agriculture and forestry.

---

[7] Fusing Self-Reported and Sensor Data from Mixed-Reality Training, *(I/ITSEC) 2014, Trevor Richardson, Stephen Gilbert, Joseph Holub, Frederick Thompson, Anastacia MacAllister, Rafael Radkowski, Eliot Winer Iowa State University, Paul Davies, Scott Terry, The Boeing Company.*
[8] Hou, Lei, *et al.,* ibid.
[9] F. Loch, F. Quint and I. Brishtel. ibid.
[10] Hou, Lei, *et al.,* ibid.
[11] Nordhaus, W. *The Sources of the Productivity Rebound and the Manufacturing Employment.* National Bureau of Economic Research, Working Paper No. 11354 May 2005. JEL No. O4, E1

i. Augmented Reality and Smart Agriculture

State-of-the-art farm management practices such as precision agriculture, site specific crop management, and Internet of Things (IoT) farming have reduced costs and improved yields for farmers around the world. Augmented Reality (AR) applications can enhance many aspects of smart agriculture by providing tools that streamline the measurement and collection of inputs, and the delivery of analysis and insights that enable data-driven decision making.

IoT smart agriculture is one of the driving forces that allows the United States to produce 7,637 kilograms of cereal per hectare, nearly twice the world average in crop yield.[12] A wide range of sensors are now being implemented: BI Intelligence predicts that IoT device installations in the agriculture world will increase from 30 million in 2015 to 75 million in 2020, a compound annual growth rate of 20 percent.[13]

Thanks in part to the steady reduction in electronics and data storage costs, a wide range of sensors are being utilized across smart agriculture including biological, chemical and gas analyzers, water sensors, meteorological sensors, weed seekers, optical cameras, Light Detection and Ranging (LIDAR), photometric sensors, soil respiration, photosynthesis sensors, Leaf Area index (LAI) sensors, range finders, Dendrometers, and hygrometers. Whether in unmanned aerial or ground vehicles (UAVs or UGVs), or stationed in the field, these IoT sensors sample, measure and collect key performance data including soil fertility diagnostics, yield as-planted, and as-applied, and water utilization. AR technology could provide additional insights into the optimization of seed, fertilizer, and chemical input, planting prescriptions, profit mapping and analysis and future crop planning.

An AR interface displayed within devices such as the DAQRI Smart Helmet can show this vital information contextually within individual management zones, with real-time data like soil moisture levels, sunlight cations, projected Nitrogen use, and other advanced analytics appearing in the wearable device's view as the farmer traverses the ground.

Augmented reality systems have been proposed for agricultural uses across the spectrum including insect identification and pest management,[14] damage level estimation of diseased plant leaves,[15] outdoor visualization of agricultural geographic information system (GIS) data,[16] and GPS guidance for agricultural tractors.[17] Additional use cases might include visualizing prescriptive planning, enabling data collection of variables such as crop yield, terrain features and topography, organic matter content, moisture levels, nitrogen levels, pH, soil electrical conductivity, magnesium, and potassium.

Many other data visualization use cases that improve decision making in real-time could be implemented, for example three-dimensional on-site visualization of topographic maps and geomatic data such as altitude, expected crop yield and actual crop yield.[18]

It is well within the capabilities of AR technology to provide farmers push notifications, with a farmer looking out over the field and red warning notifications popping up where weed, insect, disease or drought pressures pass a given threshold.

Congress and the Administration, whether through the U.S. Department of Agriculture or other Federal agencies, should provide seed money and other grants to set up field studies in this area to document the outcomes and determine how much benefit the farming community may derive from these agricultural applications of AR technology.

---

[12] Cereal yield (kg per hectare). The World Bank. Accessed from: *http://data.worldbank.org/indicator/AG.YLD.CREL.KG.* Accessed 12/18/16.

[13] Meola, Andrew. "Why IoT, Big Data & Smart Farming is the Future of Agriculture." *Business Insider.* October 7, 2016. Accessed from: *http://www.businessinsider.com/internet-of-things-smart-agriculture-2016-10.* Accessed 12/18/16.

[14] A. Nigam, P. Kabra and P. Doke, "Augmented Reality in agriculture," *2011 IEEE 7th International Conference on Wireless and Mobile Computing, Networking and Communications (WiMob),* Wuhan, 2011, pp. 445–448.

[15] S. Prasad, S. K. Peddoju and D. Ghosh, "Mobile Mixed Reality Based Damage Level Estimation of Diseased Plant Leaf," *2014 Eighth International Conference on Next Generation Mobile Apps, Services and Technologies,* Oxford, 2014, pp. 72–77.

[16] G. R. King, W. Piekarski and B. H. Thomas, "ARVino—outdoor augmented reality visualisation of viticulture GIS data," *Fourth IEEE and ACM International Symposium on Mixed and Augmented Reality (ISMAR'05),* 2005, pp. 52–55.

[17] Santana-Fernández, Javier; Gómez-Gil, Jaime; Del-Pozo-San-Cirilo, Laura. 2010. "Design and Implementation of a GPS Guidance System for Agricultural Tractors Using Augmented Reality Technology." *Sensors* 10, no. 11: 10435–10447.

[18] Goddard, Ted. "Augmented Reality Farming Geomatics." Accessed from: *https://www.youtube.com/watch?v=qrZYb5aa44k.* Accessed on 12/16/16.

ii. Augmented Reality Farm Equipment Repair & Maintenance

Augmented Reality can enhance farm operations by providing ways to improve outcomes and increase efficiency in training, maintenance, repair, and part ordering of farm machinery and equipment. Similar applications of AR as a facilitator in the maintenance of aircraft have resulted in better learning and recall, improving knowledge-transfer and training outcomes.[19] This same use of AR for airplanes can be applied to farm equipment to help farm managers monitor machine analytics, anticipate problems and analyze breakdowns quickly, reducing downtime and helping to keep planting and harvest on schedule. Moreover, this technology shows potential in reducing overall use of pesticides while targeting problem areas. It may also reduce farmers' trips to the field thanks to the increased connectedness it provides.

iii. Augmented Reality Applications in Forestry

In forestry—another key rural industry—smart IoT techniques are being utilized with the aim of controlling parameters of interest such as diameter of trees, crown height, bark thickness and other variables, such as canopy, humidity, illumination, and CO_2 transformation.

The application of wearables in forestry can be used in identifying and managing tree populations utilizing the same parameters as used in individual management zones with AR in Farming. In addition, wearables could provide first rate field training for students and new employees in real-time tree identification and other relevant facts.

IV. Augmented Reality Applications in Mining

In addition to these examples of Augmented Reality (AR) applications in rural areas, there are excellent use cases for AR in mining. Increased access to relevant real-time information saves time for workers and improves decision-making. This is one of the key benefits that AR can provide to mine workers.

Pervasive sensing—the practice of deploying large numbers of sensors and linking them to communication networks in order to analyze their collective data—is already being used in the mining industry to support remote operations, health and safety, and exploration and mapping. The identification and management of ore grade, which is relevant across all stages of the mining process, can be provided by sensing technologies during exploration, extraction, haulage and processing activities.[20] AR has been proposed as a mechanism to visualize sub-surface mining data,[21] and beyond that depth and localization data, 3D ranging and mapping, infrared data, and machine condition monitoring data are all examples of information that can be displayed in context to workers onsite using Augmented Reality head-up displays in order to improve operational efficiency and safety.

Augmented Reality can also help reduce mining accidents and lost workers. Major safety issues in the mining industry occur when personnel are in the field, such as when workers get lost underground and can no longer find their way back to the surface, or when miners encounter dangerous or explosive gases. Wearable AR devices have the additional added benefit of providing worker localization, allowing teams to remain in contact when miners lose visual contact with their teammates, and enabling the rapid localization of workers when emergency attention is needed.

V. AR in Medical Practice and Training

Augmented Reality (AR) can help American surgeons provide a greater number of procedures faster, more accurately, and more safely. The use of Augmented Reality in medicine has the potential to improve surgeon performance, reducing errors, rework, and recovery times. AR-assisted planning and navigation techniques provide the means to create detailed plans of surgical routes and then overlay 3-dimensional patient data from CT, MRI and CAT scans directly over the patient's body during the operation, guiding the procedure in a highly individualized way. These types of techniques make our medical practitioners more globally competitive, and can also directly impact the overall health and safety of the American workforce and population.

---

[19] Valimont, R. B., Gangadharan, S. N., Vincenzi, D. A., & Majoros, A. E. (2007). The Effectiveness of Augmented Reality as a Facilitator of Information Acquisition in Aviation Maintenance Applications. Journal of Aviation/Aerospace Education & Research, 16(2). Retrieved from *http://commons.erau.edu/jaaer/vol16/iss2/9.*

[20] M. E. Kiziroglou; D. E. Boyle; E. M. Yeatman; J. J. Cilliers, "Opportunities for sensing systems in mining," in *IEEE Transactions on Industrial Informatics,* vol.PP, no.99, pp.1–1.

[21] Roberts, Gethin W., *et al.,* "The use of augmented reality, GPS and INS for subsurface data visualization." FIG XXII International Congress. 2002. APA

Augmented Reality has been shown to improve medical training for surgeons.[22] We currently have a gap in the number of surgeons needed to adequately serve the population: the ratio of general surgeons per 100,000 people has dropped by 26 percent in the last 25 years. The number of general surgeons needed to adequately serve the population is estimated to be at least 7 per 100,000 people. Currently, there are about 18,000 active general surgeons in the US, or 5.8 per 100,000 people. AR can help increase the number of surgeons by making surgical training and OR operations more broadly accessible.

Question 2. In March 2016, *FedTech* magazine reported that the National Security Agency is considering the use of augmented reality applications to assist security professionals in monitoring cyber threats. How could businesses and educational institutions use similar concepts to transform cybersecurity training?

Answer. As reported by *FedTech* magazine, NSA is developing a prototype of an Augmented Reality (AR) system with the aim of helping security professionals to manage the high cognitive workload involved in processing a high volume of information flow with frequent changes in priority. Dr. Josiah Dykstra, who is leading the initiative, envisions utilizing AR to streamline task processing by surfacing the most pertinent threats immediately in a wearable, Augmented Reality head-up display.

Such a system would benefit from AR head-up-displays' capacity to highlight key information directly in the wearer's field of view, separating the signal from the noise. Security analysts responsible for areas such as intrusion detection, incident response, situational awareness, and digital forensics could benefit from this type of Augmented Reality alert. In order to function properly, the AR system would require that the most important and immediate threats are provided as an input so that they can be displayed to the wearer of the head-up display in the form of an appropriately designed AR interface. In addition to the AR-specific system components, the creation of such a system might entail the development of software algorithms that model and prioritize incoming intelligence.

Thanks to advances in commercially available Augmented Reality products, it is now feasible to design this type of overall system capable of modeling, analyzing and visualizing threats relevant to the given context. Key aspects of cybersecurity could be built into the system and highlighted through the AR interface if incidents meet a given threshold. The system could also then utilize built-in intelligence to suggest next steps or required actions.

For the purposes of training cybersecurity professionals, businesses and educational institutions could recreate the security professional's specific work environment and provide interactive real-time cyber-threat simulation in that context, while utilizing Augmented Reality head-up-displays to direct trainees' attention to what's most important in the moment. Either via in-person instructors that can see the scenario from behind a one-way mirror, or through pre-programmed software simulations, it is possible ramp up the difficulty of the simulation as needed. In situations where there are many threats being monitored simultaneously, the instructors behind the scenes could control what the trainees see and must respond to. If they respond incorrectly, a simulated security breach could occur, providing a valuable learning opportunity to practice incident response procedures.

Wearable augmented reality head-up displays used during the training to disseminate information about the most critical security threats could also provide guidance on follow-up procedures, and enable collaboration through process tracking and ticketing tools.

Augmented Reality (AR) can also be utilized by educational institutions earlier on in the process to generate and nurture interest from the next generation of cybersecurity professionals. Educational serious games utilizing Augmented Reality have been shown to increase awareness of cybersecurity vulnerabilities and improve defense preparation against ever-present cybersecurity threats including identity theft, oversharing, malware, and social engineering. AR in this context provides the benefit of making abstract cybersecurity concepts more tangible, and thereby allows students to interact with them directly.[23]

---

[22] Training for Planning Tumour Resection: Augmented Reality and Human Factors

[23] M. Salazar, J. Gaviria, C. Laorden and P. G. Bringas, "Enhancing cybersecurity learning through an augmented reality-based serious game," *2013 IEEE Global Engineering Education Conference (EDUCON)*, Berlin, 2013, pp. 602–607

Question 3. Many of the members of the Commerce Committee represent rural states. Are there applications of AR technology that could specifically benefit rural industries, such as agriculture?

Answer.

I. Augmented Reality and Smart Agriculture

State-of-the-art farm management practices such as precision agriculture, site specific crop management, and Internet of Things (IoT) farming have reduced costs and improved yields for farmers around the world. Augmented Reality (AR) applications can enhance many aspects of smart agriculture by providing tools that streamline the measurement and collection of inputs, and the delivery of analysis and insights that enable data-driven decision making.

IoT smart agriculture is one of the driving forces that allows the United States to produce 7,637 kilograms of cereal per hectare, nearly twice the world average in crop yield.[24] A wide range of sensors are now being implemented: BI Intelligence predicts that IoT device installations in the agriculture world will increase from 30 million in 2015 to 75 million in 2020, a compound annual growth rate of 20 percent.[25]

Thanks in part to the steady reduction in electronics and data storage costs, a wide range of sensors are being utilized across smart agriculture including biological, chemical and gas analyzers, water sensors, meteorological sensors, weed seekers, optical cameras, Light Detection and Ranging (LIDAR), photometric sensors, soil respiration, photosynthesis sensors, Leaf Area index (LAI) sensors, range finders, Dendrometers, and hygrometers. Whether in unmanned aerial or ground vehicles (UAVs or UGVs), or stationed in the field, these IoT sensors sample, measure and collect key performance data including soil fertility diagnostics, yield as-planted, and as-applied, and water utilization. AR technology could provide additional insights into the optimization of seed, fertilizer, and chemical input, planting prescriptions, profit mapping and analysis and future crop planning.

An AR interface displayed within devices such as the DAQRI Smart Helmet can show this vital information contextually within individual management zones, with real-time data like soil moisture levels, sunlight cations, projected Nitrogen use, and other advanced analytics appearing in the wearable device's view as the farmer traverses the ground.

Augmented reality systems have been proposed for agricultural uses across the spectrum including insect identification and pest management,[26] damage level estimation of diseased plant leaves,[27] outdoor visualization of agricultural geographic information system (GIS) data,[28] and GPS guidance for agricultural tractors.[29] Additional use cases might include visualizing prescriptive planning, enabling data collection of variables such as crop yield, terrain features and topography, organic matter content, moisture levels, nitrogen levels, pH, soil electrical conductivity, magnesium, and potassium.

Many other data visualization use cases that improve decision making in real-time could be implemented, for example three-dimensional on-site visualization of topographic maps and geomatic data such as altitude, expected crop yield and actual crop yield.[30]

It is well within the capabilities of AR technology to provide farmers push notifications, with a farmer looking out over the field and red warning notifications popping up where weed, insect, disease or drought pressures pass a given threshold.

---

[24] Cereal yield (kg per hectare). The World Bank. http://data.worldbank.org/indicator/AG.YLD.CREL.KG. Accessed 12/18/16.

[25] Meola, Andrew. "Why IoT, Big Data & Smart Farming is the Future of Agriculture." *Business Insider.* October 7, 2016. *http://www.businessinsider.com/internet-of-things-smart-agriculture-2016–10.* Accessed 12/18/16.

[26] A. Nigam, P. Kabra and P. Doke, "Augmented Reality in agriculture," *2011 IEEE 7th International Conference on Wireless and Mobile Computing, Networking and Communications (WiMob),* Wuhan, 2011, pp. 445–448.

[27] S. Prasad, S. K. Peddoju and D. Ghosh, "Mobile Mixed Reality Based Damage Level Estimation of Diseased Plant Leaf," *2014 Eighth International Conference on Next Generation Mobile Apps, Services and Technologies,* Oxford, 2014, pp. 72–77.

[28] G. R. King, W. Piekarski and B. H. Thomas, "ARVino—outdoor augmented reality visualisation of viticulture GIS data," *Fourth IEEE and ACM International Symposium on Mixed and Augmented Reality (ISMAR'05),* 2005, pp. 52–55.

[29] Santana-Fernández, Javier; Gómez-Gil, Jaime; Del-Pozo-San-Cirilo, Laura. 2010. "Design and Implementation of a GPS Guidance System for Agricultural Tractors Using Augmented Reality Technology." *Sensors* 10, no. 11: 10435–10447.

[30] Goddard, Ted. "Augmented Reality Farming Geomatics." Retried from: *https://www.youtube.com/watch?v=qrZYb5aa44k*

Congress and the Administration, whether through the U.S. Department of Agriculture or other Federal agencies, should provide seed money and other grants to set up field studies in this area to document the outcomes and determine how much benefit the farming community may derive from these agricultural applications of AR technology.

II. Augmented Reality Farm Equipment Repair & Maintenance

Augmented Reality can enhance farm operations by providing ways to improve outcomes and increase efficiency in training, maintenance, repair, and part ordering of farm machinery and equipment. Similar applications of AR as a facilitator in the maintenance of aircraft have resulted in better learning and recall, improving knowledge-transfer and training outcomes.[31] This same use of AR for airplanes can be applied to farm equipment to help farm managers monitor machine analytics, anticipate problems and analyze breakdowns quickly, reducing downtime and helping to keep planting and harvest on schedule. Moreover, this technology shows potential in reducing overall use of pesticides while targeting problem area. It may also reduce farmers trips to the field.

III. Augmented Reality Applications in Forestry

In forestry—another key rural industry—smart IoT techniques are being utilized with the aim of controlling parameters of interest such as diameter of trees, crown height, bark thickness and other variables, such as canopy, humidity, illumination, and CO_2 transformation.

The application of wearables in forestry can be used in identifying and managing tree populations utilizing the same parameters as used in individual management zones with AR in Farming. In addition, wearables could provide first rate field training for students and new employees in real-time tree identification and other relevant facts.

———

RESPONSE TO WRITTEN QUESTIONS SUBMITTED BY HON. MARCO RUBIO TO BRIAN MULLINS

Question 1. As we conduct our oversight role as lawmakers, how can we ensure that technology start-ups, like Magic Leap, are able to continue to advance in the 21st century economy without imposing unnecessary red tape?

Answer. Some regulation and oversight are needed to ensure that innovative technologies created by start-ups do not harm the public. However, due to the rapid speed of innovation in the technology industry, there are many cases where reactive laws attempting to regulate emerging technologies have been rendered obsolete in a short span of time. Worse, broad brush regulations can have unintended side effects and stifle technology development that actually increases safety and improves lives. In the case of Augmented Reality (AR) technologies, lawmakers should consider and be aware of the wide variety of use cases beyond consumer-oriented gaming, social media, and entertainment, which will require a very different analysis. For example, during the hearing on 11/16/16, a question was posed on whether AR technology was unsafe for use in automobiles. While the Senator was referring to the playing of interactive games while driving—which is clearly unsafe and may warrant regulation—there are other uses of AR technology in automobiles which actually increase safety, such as head-up displays which project information such as the odometer or driving directions directly onto the wind screen so that the driver is no longer forced to take his or her eyes off the road, even for a second or two. As we have expressed in answers to the jobs-related questions from this committee, AR provides significant benefits in terms of worker safety and productivity in a wide variety of fields. Through the minimization of errors and the reduction of cognitive load, AR can significantly improve the quality and safety of not just the work environment, but also the end products, such as industrial equipment, consumer goods, infrastructure and construction projects, and so on. These improvements in turn benefit the American public at large, who are the beneficiaries, users, and inhabitants of the final outputs of the AR-enhanced production process. Currently, the aerospace, energy, construction, manufacturing, automotive and utilities industries are leading the way in AR implementation on the factory floor and in the

---

[31] Valimont, R. B., Gangadharan, S. N., Vincenzi, D. A., & Majoros, A. E. (2007). The Effectiveness of Augmented Reality as a Facilitator of Information Acquisition in Aviation Maintenance Applications. Journal of Aviation/Aerospace Education & Research, 16(2). Retrieved from *http://commons.erau.edu/jaaer/vol16/iss2/9*

field, and adoption is on the rise as highly functional and robust AR devices are becoming more widely available.

Augmented Reality applications have safety benefits for both the workers that produce and the end users that come into contact with a wide range of goods, ranging from aircraft to chemical plants. These types of applications require the use of data capture and storage technologies, but in industrial rather than consumer contexts. It's important to consider the vast differences in AR use for consumers versus industry use cases. We posit that lawmakers can protect consumers and data privacy through regulations that empower people to have control of their own data, while still enabling industrial usage that will improve worker safety and American competitiveness.

Tech start-ups are small businesses. Looking more broadly across the start-up ecosystem, we recommend not enacting laws that make it too cumbersome to be a small tech company. For example, it might be worthwhile to find ways to allow small businesses to enter government contracting by either providing case-by-case exemptions to FAR/D–FARS or by creating other programs that allow them to participate in government grant and research programs. Too many rules and regulations create a situation where it is not feasible economically for small tech firms to participate in government contracting, preventing the government's ability to leverage new innovations. When creating new laws, we ask that you consider the potential unintended consequences of new regulations on small companies in emerging markets. If you truly want to have more diversity and the kind of disruptive innovation that's possible with start-ups, the rules of engagement need to allow more flexibility and more competition, which will improve the end-products that can ultimately support government people, goals, and functions. Without start-ups at the table, we will risk getting stuck with a glacial pace of change, and inefficient cost-plus models. Conversely, government runs the risk of not having a voice in start-up driven conversations regarding the most important disruptive innovations of the future.

One issue that affects all technology companies is the scourge of patent trolls: bad actors who do not add value to the economy nor enhance current technologies but instead distract and slow down the real innovators in the marketplace through unwarranted and expensive legal action. Regulations that put a stop to patent trolls would be welcomed by start-ups and large tech businesses alike.

Question 2. In your opinion, would current regulations placed on the gaming and computer industry be appropriate to apply to this new generation technology?

Answer. States across the U.S. are trying to determine how to regulate new technologies that collect data about our health; track our movements and monitor our homes or workplaces. Currently, there is a patchwork of laws and regulations that attempt to deal with emerging technologies. Most focus primarily on safety, and we understand the need to design our products and AR experiences to address additional concerns about privacy, usability and affordability for all, and cybersecurity.

AR products and services allow data to flow real time between users, their environment and data collection. While this type of communication allows for enhanced safety, particularly in the workplace, we are sensitive to the fact that users need to be made aware of what data is collected; how it is collected; how it will be used/ shared and stored. We have given great thought to this issue to ensure our cus- tomers understand the flow of data associated with our products and ensure they have consented to such collection and use.

DAQRI's stance is that Augmented Reality (AR) applications for industrial, automotive and consumer use should each be treated differently. As we've discussed in response to other questions from this committee, industrial applications of AR in many industries from energy to manufacturing to aerospace have been shown to increase safety, productivity and efficiency. These benefits must be weighed when considering new regulations that might restrict usage or delivery of Augmented Reality in any way.

In the automotive field, current regulations enable and require safety features for driving, an activity that is fundamental to so many lives. Head-up-displays have been shown to reduce blind flight time of drivers.[32] Due to the significant safety benefits, lawmakers should consider how we can expand the capability and adoption of AR HUDs.

Question 3. Autism is an issue I feel very passionate about and have worked on going back to my time in the Florida legislature. Some have suggested that augmented reality games can benefit people on the autism spectrum in terms of getting

---

[32] R. J. Kiefer and A. W. Gellatly, "Quantifying the Consequences of the 'Eyes-on-Road' Benefit Attributed to Head-Up Displays," p. 960946, Feb. 1996.

them out of the house and developing their social skills. Is the industry doing any of its own scientific research to determine the actual benefits of augmented gaming to people on the autism spectrum?

Answer. There have been numerous studies performed over recent years on the benefits that augmented reality (AR) technology can provide to individuals on the autism spectrum. These studies have demonstrated how AR can positively impact their lives by improving several aspects of social behavior including but not limited to: the frequency and depth of social interactions, the reduction in social slipups, more seamless group integration, an increased selective attention span, and a boost in overall motivation to engage.[1]

Many see even greater promise in the potential of AR than in more widely adopted computer learning aids for autism, an area that has been thoroughly studied and has seen much success over the years. The abundant use of engaging visuals offered by mobile AR devices allows for real-time feedback in a natural setting, increasing the likelihood of generalization. For example, mobile assistance tools, such as the Mobile Social Compass (MOSOCO), can offer a variety of interactive features to aid in enhancing social and functional skills. MOSOCO was deployed during a study at a public school in Southern California and through its guidance, children with autism were provided with "interactive features to encourage them to make eye contact, maintain appropriate spatial boundaries, reply to conversation initiators, share interests with partners, disengage appropriately at the end of an interaction, and identify potential communication partners." The results of the study demonstrated that the AR tool could increase both the quantity and quality of social interactions, reduce social and behavioral missteps, and enable the integration of children with autism into social groups of neurotypical children.[33]

Furthermore, these mobile tools can be tailored to each individual case, as individuals fall on different levels of the autism scale and need varying levels of support.[34] Researchers believe that educational AR tools, such as MOSOCO, that have prospered within the boundaries of the classroom can also provide adequate mobile assistance to people on the autism scale in real-life scenarios.[1]

An additional study titled, *Augmented Reality for Rehabilitation of Cognitive Disabled Children: A Preliminary Study,* demonstrates such promise when using an ARVe (Augmented Reality applied to the Vegetal field) system as a teaching aid to support a task that involves pairing fruits, leaves, stems, and seeds. By overlaying 2D and 3D objects on printed-square markers in the form of a book, children were able to interact with objects in a non-immersive and intuitive manner. This application integrated visual, olfactory, or auditory cues to help children carry out the decision making process. Researchers noted that, "in the ARVe application, matching is an activity that the autistic children like because their visual aptitude is used for a precise goal, with some discovery pleasure and curiosity that are sources of motivation for these children." Researchers recognized that, "given the possibility of adjusting the task, the AR tool is valuable to offer to the cognitive disabled pupils the same training as the other pupils of the elementary cycle." Parents of the children were supportive as well, with 90 percent positively favoring the study, emphasizing that the tools could involve their children in a much deeper learning process.[35]

What's more, several studies have shown a correlation between the adoption of educational AR tools over traditional learning methods and an increase in motivation, focus, positive emotion, and sustained attention. While using Mobis, a tool that allowed teachers to superimpose digital content on physical objects, autistic students experienced a 24 percent increase in positive emotion, a 20 percent increase in time spent on an individual task, a 62 percent increase in selective attention, and a 45 percent increase in sustained attention.[36]

These are just a few examples of studies demonstrating how AR can positively impact the lives of those who are affected with autism. From increasing selective attention and motivation to helping to socially integrate kids with autism at school, the effects of AR have endless possibilities.

---

[33] Escobedo, Lizbeth, David Nguyen, LouAnne Boyd3, Sen H. Hirano, Alejandro Rangel, Daniel Garc'ia-Rosas1, Monica Tentori, and Gillian R. Hayes. MOSOCO: A Mobile Assistive Tool to Support Children with Autism Practicing Social Skills in Real-Life Situations. Gillian Hayes. N.p., Aug. 2012. Web. 19 Dec. 2016.
[34] "DSM–5 Diagnostic Criteria." Autism Speaks. N.p., n.d. Web. 19 Dec. 2016.
[35] E. Richard, V. Billaudeau, P. Richard and G. Gaudin, "Augmented Reality for Rehabilitation of Cognitive Disabled Children: A Preliminary Study," *2007 Virtual Rehabilitation*, Venice, Italy, 2007, pp. 102–108.
[36] Escobedo, Lizbeth, Monica Tentori, Eduardo Quintana, Jesus Favela, and Daniel Garcia-Rosas. "Using Augmented Reality to Help Children with Autism Stay Focused." IEEE Pervasive Computing 13.1 (2014): 38–46. Web. 19 Dec. 2016.

Question 4. What would you say our high schools and universities can be doing better in the coming years to ensure that people in Florida and in the United States acquire the skills and preparation to fill these jobs?

Answer.

Augmented Reality systems leverage many technologies

State-of-the-art Augmented Reality (AR) systems require the integration of a wide range of technical disciplines: computer vision tracking, high-speed graphical rendering, electronic and optical engineering, and low-latency cloud computing to name a few. Implementation of an AR solution in a specific context such a factory, or integrated into a larger system such as a passenger vehicle, requires additional layers of systems engineering and information technology expertise, such as networking, data analytics, and cybersecurity. In the midst of all this complexity, all sub-systems must work together to support the goals of the larger whole. Given this context, both deep domain expertise and big picture thinking are required for success.

AR experiences require creative disciplines

A well-designed AR interface requires the extreme application of user-centric design, given the proximity and personalization of an interface that sits directly in one's field of view. It is more crucial than ever to consider and understand human factors in the design of Augmented Reality interfaces, applications, and products. For this reason, creative professionals who can create functional designs that people love to use are always in very high demand in the AR industry. In addition to having a strong skillset in design thinking, creatives also need to deeply understand how the underlying technology works, in order to be able to innovative and push the boundaries of its capabilities.

The role of educational institutions

The best thing that educational institutions can do is to integrate AR in the classroom in high school and even before. Not only will it improve learning outcomes, it will also prepare the next generation to work in one of the most exciting industries of our time. If we do not take this opportunity, we run the risk of falling behind in a global context.

Furthermore, high schools and universities can and should do more to promote STEM and design thinking education in our schools, but that alone is not enough. Educators can instill the habit of multi-disciplinary thinking bigger in students through the implementation of entrepreneurship programs, project-based learning methods, and the integration of agile methodologies. When students have the opportunity to create end-to-end solutions it more realistically prepares them for real-world, provides greater motivation to engage, and enables them to keep the bigger picture in mind. Students who have taken a project from zero to launch have greater job prospects in a market that is increasingly seeking problem solvers with entrepreneurial skillsets.

AR is inspirational precisely because it is so technically challenging across STEM disciplines and so broadly applicable in all areas of human activity—from building airplanes and rockets to interactive mobile gaming. Teachers and educational institutions can engage students more fully by building on the excitement for a subject that is so fundamentally cool.

Question 5. What message would you like to send to educators and students alike about the industry's future and the opportunities it presents?

Answer. Augmented Reality is an extremely exciting field for students to pursue. Not only is it one of the fastest growing technologies in the history of the world, but like the Internet, it has the potential to touch every other industry.

Unlike most industries, our educational system has struggled to evolve over time. The setup and structure of classrooms today mirror those of 100 years ago. This antiquated design can limit a student's ability to express knowledge in creative and innovative ways, forcing them to conform to the status quo. It's time that changes. Our high schools and universities must provide a student-directed learning environment that encourages students to take risks, learn from setbacks and failures along the way, and ignore society's limitations. We need to ensure students can still dream of a better world if we're to have any hope of living in one.

Futurist Thomas Frey predicts 60 percent of the jobs 10 years from now haven't been invented yet [37] and those that have been invented will be drastically different

---

[37]Thomas Frey, futurist. Accessed from: *http://www.futuristspeaker.com/business-trends/55-jobs-of-the-future/*.Accessed 12/19/16.

due to technological advances. Our schools can prepare students for the future of work by instilling the value of lifelong learning; designing curriculum where students learn through discovery and creation, not consumption, and provide a culture where your results matter just as much as how you treat the people around you. The Augmented Reality industry provides students with the exciting opportunity to contribute to a new frontier of technology innovation. This opportunity will require a workforce that dreams without limitations and a passion for pushing the boundaries of the newest technologies. Augmented reality will empower students as much as computer skills in previous decades, and will prove to be a differentiator in the way we experience life.

Question 6. The interface created by these new technologies can be a tremendous asset to the Department of Defense, especially for training. How can the Department of Defense collaborate with innovators to push the limits of mixed reality technologies to ensure our men and women in uniform continue to be the best trained and equipped fighting force on this Earth?

Answer. Augmented Reality (AR) technology can serve as a force multiplier in defense training and operations by increasing situational awareness, reducing the fog of war, counteracting information overload, improving targeting cycle times, and enhancing battlefield collaboration.[38] Airforce fighter pilots have long benefitted from AR interfaces in head-up displays that superimpose information from a variety of data streams, including targets, navigation waypoints, and threats, over their 3D locations. By providing virtual overlays that seamlessly merge mission critical information into pilots' field of vision, AR allows pilots to keep their eyes on the real environment, improving reaction time, and reducing cognitive load.

Our men and women in uniform on land and at sea can benefit from the same advantages AR provides to pilots. In 2014, DAQRI entered into a cooperative research and development agreement (CRADA) with the Space and Naval Warfare Systems Command (SPAWAR) to explore and measure the benefits of augmented reality (AR) tools for Naval applications and to support the development of new capabilities for the Navy.

In the first quarter of 2016, a coalition of Naval commands met on USS Essex to launch the first platform for Sailors to bring innovative technological concepts straight from the deckplates to Navy labs for rapid prototyping and testing in the fleet. Navy leadership spoke at the Innovation Jam, encouraging sailors to "be bold and bring forth ideas and solutions to fleet challenges," [39] and also served as judges as six Sailor finalists pitched technological solutions, with two winners receiving funds and support to build prototypes. LT Robert McClenning from USS Gridley was selected as the winner and received prototyping funds for his Unified Gunnery System concept which featured an augmented reality helmet that would fuse information from the gunnery officer and weapon system into an easy-to-interpret visual format for the gunner manning a naval gun system.

Through the collaboration with SPAWAR, DAQRI partnered with the Navy's Battlefield Exploitation of Mixed Reality (BEMR) Laboratory [40] to develop and demonstrate LT McClenning's prototype Augmented Reality command and control concept. Christened GunnAR, the application leverages the DAQRI Smart Helmet as a wearable augmented reality display and enables the issuing of commands by the gunnery officer to gunners aboard Navy ships, which then are shown directly in the field of view of the targeting officer and all gunnery positions. If implemented at scale, this system could greatly improve the targeting cycle and shipboard situational awareness. Many small caliber engagements occur close to shore or near ports, so improving the targeting officers' ability to control fires could significantly reduce friendly fire incidents.

We hope to work with the Office of Naval Research and other DOD research centers to ensure prototype systems like GunnAR are funded, developed, and deployed to the fleet, cementing a battlefield edge that no opponent will have.

Beyond being an exceptional training aid, AR could one day provide every soldier with a common operating picture of the battle space and deliver an unmatched competitive edge. To ensure that the Department of Defense can implement the mixed reality advances being achieved in the commercial world, we respectfully request consideration of the following:

---

[38] Livingston, M.; Rosenblum, L.; Brown, G.; Schmidt, G; Julier, S.; Baillot, Y.; Swan II, J.; Ai, Z.; Maassel, P. *Military Applications of Augmented Reality,* chapter in Handbook of Augmented Reality pp 671–706. Date: 13 July 2011.

[39] *Inaugural Innovation Jam Funds Sailor-Driven Improvements, http://www.navy.mil/submit/display.asp?story∎ id=93698,* accessed 12/14/16.

[40] *Battlefield Exploitation of Mixed Reality (BEMR) Laboratory, http://www.public.navy.mil/spawar/Pacific/BEMR/Pages/default.aspx,* accessed 12/14/16.

I. Fund studies for design, development and demonstration of military-specific AR applications using COTS systems that demonstrate improvement of battlefield situational awareness, which would lead over time to military-specific hardware and software solutions that will give our soldiers a force multiplier that no opponent will have.

II. Increase programs that encourage and enable collaboration between the military and commercial innovators such as cooperative research and development agreements (CRADAs) and JIDO's Hacking4Defense—a model based upon Silicon Valley's lean and agile innovation methodology.

III. Increase programs that support internal innovation so that our men and women in uniform can come up with great ideas and pull innovation out of the commercial space. The Navy's Innovation Jam, The Hatch, and The Bridge are commendable examples. The 140,000 members of the fleet have many good ideas and bright people but are stifled by procedure and systems of record that prevent them from solving problems in an agile manner.

IV. Improve the ability for innovators to develop products for the military and feel confident that their IP will not be put at risk. This is particularly important if the DOD is going to leverage the most advanced technology that is funded by start-up investors and high tech companies that currently have a primary focus on commercial business. Allowing companies to continue to develop technology and more easily navigate through export control issues, *e.g.,* ITAR, will support companies by allowing them to add DOD business development and engineering focus to DOD applications without fear that their core IP will be shared or put at risk in a way that is outside the company's control.

As mixed reality technologies have matured over the last fifteen years, explorations of augmented and virtual reality defense applications have correspondingly increased. Since the year 2000, the U.S. Naval Research Laboratory has published over 50 papers describing the development and testing of a Battlefield Augmented Reality System (BARS) and the capabilities it imparts or enhances including X-ray vision and depth perception, information filtering, collaboration, and embedded training.[41]

Other defense applications of COTS Augmented Reality innovation

It is crucial to enable military applications of the most advanced innovations available in emerging technology, which today are often originate in the commercial sector.

For example, the *Augmented Immersion Team Training* [42] (AITT) system, developed by the Marine Corps and supported by the Office of Naval Research, was demonstrated in 2015. Through AR, AITT provides more realistic force-on-force ground training for small unit leaders, forward observers, and mortarmen, resulting in improved effectiveness and efficiency. Combining hardware and software components, AITT utilizes a commercial-off-the-shelf (COTS) head-worn display and tactical equipment such as binoculars to overlay realistic virtual elements onto real world landscapes. A wide array of virtual elements can be simulated including weapons, artillery and mortar effects, fixed and rotary wing aircraft, and targets such as enemy personnel, tanks and buildings, creating a more realistic training environment at a fraction of the cost of live training.

In 2015, Lockheed Martin and SRI International presented an augmented reality-based vehicle training system for tactical and gunnery training that simulated realistic and responsive training targets. Instructor software enabled instructors to run scenarios that resemble live fire training events without much of the associated costs and risks and allowing trainee performance statistics to be gathered.[43] The AR system was tested on an Army Stryker operating in real range and coordinated simulations between the Styker's three driver periscopes, the gunner's remote weapons system (RWS), and the fire control unit (FCU), enabling real-time team collaboration. Much of the research literature on Augmented Reality takes the position that AR's potential will be fully realizable when highly robust and functional hardware is widely commercially available. Finally, these capabilities can now be supported

[41] Julier, S; Baillot, Y; Lanzagorta, M; Brown, D; Rosenblum, L. "Bars: Battlefield augmented reality system." *In NATO Symposium on Information Processing Techniques for Military Systems.* 2000.

[42] *Augmented Immersion Team Training, http://www.onr.navy.mil/Media-Center/Fact-Sheets/AITT.aspx,* accessed 12/14/16.

[43] Brookshire, J.; Oskiper, T.; *et al.,* Military Vehicle Training with Augmented Reality. Interservice/Industry Training, Simulation, and Education Conference, November, 2015.

by commercial-off-the-shelf AR hardware designed for use in industrial environments.

Question 7. In your testimony you stated, "Technology can take away jobs. It's true though that most times when it does, it creates new, even better jobs." Can you speak to how the expansion of AR technology will create "new, even better jobs" in the transportation, construction, defense, training and manufacturing sectors?
Answer.

Technology's impact on jobs

When it comes to employment, the painful consequences of disruptive technology are more readily felt in the short term than the opportunities generated by rapid innovation, and often receive the lion's share of public attention. However, economic research shows that new technologies create many more jobs than are lost, and in the process create auxiliary economic benefits such as consumer surplus, greater variety and consumer choice, and increased convenience. Over the past 15 years, the Internet created 2.6 new jobs globally for every job it eliminated. This growth occurred mainly through the modernization of traditional activities: 75 percent of the economic impact came from companies who define themselves as traditional firms. Since Augmented Reality is a communication medium that connects people to information in a new way, it shares some characteristics with the World Wide Web, including the potential to touch nearly every traditional industry.

Historically, the benefits of innovation have not been evenly distributed, especially for displaced employees who are older or have less formal education. Augmented Reality can help level the playing field for American workers and empower them to stay ahead of the curve in a shifting technological landscape—but before we turn to this topic let's look at two examples of related technologies that have had a net positive impact on job growth.

Augmented reality is closely tied to the growing Industrial Internet of Things (IIoT), which is expected to create new jobs in industrial data science, robotics, IT solution architecture, industrial computer programming, and industrial UI/UX design, among other areas. At a macroeconomic level, the IIoT is powering the growing trend toward the outcome economy, where organizations shift their focus from the provision of products to the delivery of measurable outcomes important to the customer.[44] A significant factor in new job creation in traditional industries is exactly this type of new business model enablement. From 2004 to 2014, manufacturing jobs declined by 2 million, while services jobs have increased by 10 million.[45] Traditional businesses like General Electric are hiring thousands of software engineers to provide software and data services.[46]

Augmented Reality job creation in manufacturing: The Industrial Internet of Things and the link between productivity and employment

One of the main driving forces behind the high demand for Augmented Reality (AR) applications in manufacturing is the capacity of AR to serve as the user interface for the Industrial Internet of Things (IIoT), displaying relevant sensor data, trends, and control information directly in the field of view of the worker on the factory floor. AR implementations in industrial contexts will create a range of new jobs including hardware and software systems integrators, data analysts, interface designers, trainers, and AR project managers.

At a macroeconomic level, Augmented Reality is likely to increase demand for manufacturing jobs due to its ability to directly improve manufacturing productivity. As mentioned above, Augmented Reality technology delivers significant improvements in worker productivity in the context of manufacturing and assembly.[47] This higher growth in manufacturing productivity, however, does not lead to a decline in employment. According to research by Yale Economics Professor William Nordhaus, the empirical evidence shows that "rapid productivity growth leads to increased rather than decreased employment in manufacturing," as increased produc-

---

[44] Industrial Internet of Things: Unleashing the Potential of Connected Products and Services. *http://reports.weforum.org/industrial-internet-of-things/3-convergence-on-the-outcome-economy/*. World Economic Forum. See section 3.2: The emergence of the outcome economy. Accessed 12/16/16.
[45] Employment by major industry sector, Bureau of Labor Statistics. Accessed from: *https://www.bls.gov/emp/ep▮table▮201.htm#1*
[46] Power, B. Building a Software Start-Up Inside GE. *https://hbr.org/2015/01/building-a-software-start-up-inside-ge*. Accessed 12/16/16.
[47] Hou, Lei, *et al.,* "Using animated augmented reality to cognitively guide assembly." *Journal of Computing in Civil Engineering* 27.5 (2013): 439–451.

tivity leads to lower prices, thereby expanding demand, which results in increased employment.[48]

Manual work is and will continue to be a cornerstone of the economy, even as new technologies transform work environments from farming to the factory floor. However, there is a shortage of skilled workers in various manufacturing contexts. In addition to the macroeconomic dynamic explained above, Augmented Reality can help bridge the gap between unskilled workers and unmet demand for labor at a microeconomic level. For example, it has been shown that AR can help novice welders rapidly ramp up their skillset by superimposing an auxiliary visual signal directly in their line of sight over the weld pool image. Building upon a machine learning algorithm that calculates the optimal welding speed, the AR interface displays arrows with direction and amplitude, enabling trainees to make adjustments.[49] For a broader range of skillsets, it has been shown that AR assistance systems significantly reduce errors, speed, and mental workload involved in manual assembly tasks, resulting in the ability to rapidly train workers and ramp up operations.[50]

I. Augmented Reality job creation in construction, transportation, defense, and training

The "relative demand for educated workers"

Historical evidence from the decades prior to the Internet boom shows that new technology increased the relative demand for more educated workers, but only for a limited time. Echoing the healthcare example above, Ann Bartel's 1985 empirical study for the National Bureau of Economic Research found that "the relative demand for educated workers declines as the capital stock (and presumably the technology embodied therein) ages" and that "the education-distribution of employment depends . . . strongly on the age of equipment" suggesting that as new technologies become more integrated into everyday business operations, opportunities for all skill ranges increase.[51] The same study found that "the effect of changes in equipment age on labor demand is magnified in R&D-intensive industries," with the converse thus being true in less R&D intensive industries such as transportation and construction. If learning curves develop more rapidly, then the demand for less educated workers comes into play even more quickly after the introduction of new technologies.

Augmented reality improves learning curves, making labor more portable

In a 2013 study titled *Using Animated Augmented Reality to Cognitively Guide Assembly,* researchers showed not only that AR enabled improved accuracy and reduction in errors in assembly tasks, but also improved novices' learning curves.[52] This has been shown in many different environments including in surgical planning and training, where AR interfaces have been shown to improve performance in complex spatial reasoning tasks.[53]

As referenced by our written testimony to this committee on November 16, 2016, Boeing and Iowa State University's study, Augmented Reality work instructions improve accuracy, speed, focus and worker satisfaction when utilized in the training and operation of complex manufacturing tasks.[54]

[48] Nordhaus, W. *The Sources of the Productivity Rebound and the Manufacturing Employment.* National Bureau of Economic Research, Working Paper No. 11354 May 2005. JEL No. O4, E1

[49] Y. Liu and Y. Zhang, "Super welder in augmented reality welder training system: A predictive control approach," *2015 IEEE 24th International Symposium on Industrial Electronics (ISIE),* Buzios, 2015, pp. 131–136.

[50] F. Loch, F. Quint and I. Brishtel, "Comparing Video and Augmented Reality Assistance in Manual Assembly," *2016 12th International Conference on Intelligent Environments (IE),* London, 2016, pp. 147–150.

[51] Bartel, A.; Lichtenberg, F. *The Comparative Advantage of Educated Workers in Implementing New Technology: Some Empirical Evidence.* National Bureau of Economic Research, Working Paper No. 1718. October 1985.

[52] Hou, Lei, ibid.

[53] K. Abhari *et al.,* "Training for Planning Tumour Resection: Augmented Reality and Human Factors," in *IEEE Transactions on Biomedical Engineering,* vol. 62, no. 6, pp. 1466–1477, June 2015.

[54] 1 Fusing Self-Reported and Sensor Data from Mixed-Reality Training, *(I/ITSEC) 2014, Trevor Richardson, Stephen Gilbert, Joseph Holub, Frederick Thompson, Anastacia MacAllister, Rafael Radkowski, Eliot Winer Iowa State University, Paul Davies, Scott Terry, The Boeing Company*

How augmented reality levels the playing field for American workers

So far, we've argued that augmented reality improves productivity, which in turn increases employment by reducing costs and increasing demand. We've also shown that introducing new technologies into the workplace increase employment of mid-skilled workers by generating efficiencies through on-the-job experience that open up new business models, also increasing demand and thereby increasing employment. Thanks to AR's ability to significantly improve learning curves, it will decrease relative demand for highly skilled workers and increase demand for less educated segments of the workforce.

In our written testimony, we discussed how AR can empower workers to keep up with the rapidly changing pace of technology. When American workers can utilize Augmented Reality interfaces to rapidly learn, re-skill, and become cross-functionally proficient, it will transform the economy and dramatically reduce unemployment, eliminating mismatches between job vacancies and worker skillsets. AR allows those who are less formally educated to be trained (or re-trained) more quickly, more efficiently and less expensively, thereby reducing the uneven distribution of the benefits of innovation.

In order for Augmented Reality to function well in the transportation, construction, defense, training and manufacturing sectors a whole range of infrastructure and services are required:

1. Software Engineers
2. AR Hardware Engineers
3. AR Content Developers
4. Data Analysts
5. User Experience Designers
6. Product and Project Managers
7. Security and Networking Engineers

When new Internet-connected technologies are introduced, the obvious place to look for job creation is in roles related to hardware and software procurement and implementation, training, content development, integration, and networking and security, and data storage.

AR job creation and economic transformation

Augmented reality will certainly directly create those types of new jobs, but it will also have an indirect effect on the job market that is unique. Because AR can enhance the ability to rapidly understand, synthesize, and communicate new ideas, it enables workers to adapt to rapid change in the world of work. As we said in our initial testimony, AR technology allows you to overlay information into the real world and rapidly transfer knowledge that empowers workers.

The United States has always been the central player in the Internet economy: the U.S. captured more than 30 percent of global Internet revenues and more than 40 percent of net income as of 2011.[55] The American economy as a whole can maintain its competitiveness by staying ahead of game-changing technologies like AR.

---

[55] Pélissié du Rausas, ibid.

RESPONSE TO WRITTEN QUESTION SUBMITTED BY HON. JOE MANCHIN TO
BRIAN MULLINS

Question. As a former Governor and in my role as a United States Senator, I have remained committed to enhancing the job climate in my state so that West Virginians have good paying jobs and the skills to compete in the global economy. Part of this job growth is going to come from the technology sector. We are beginning to see an uptick in technology startups in different parts of the state, but I believe there are opportunities for tools such as augmented reality to enhance workforce training.

The technological advancements of the 21st century should not leave rural communities behind, and as West Virginia continues to develop its technology sector and train its workforce: How can augmented reality be used to train workers in the digital economy?

Answer.

I. Augmented Reality-based workforce training will prepare workers, across age groups and level of formal education, to compete and win in the global economy

Augmented Reality (AR) is a game-changer for job training and on-the-job skill acquisition. Three decades of research supports the conclusion that AR improves learning, productivity, accuracy, efficiency, and job satisfaction in a variety of contexts including manufacturing,[1,2] defense,[3] aerospace,[4] construction,[5] medicine[6] and other sectors.

AR technology empowers experts and novices alike to quickly learn new skills or be trained in a new area or sector—a particularly important benefit for workers who have lost their jobs and cannot easily find work in their current industry. For example, AR-based workforce training can assist a laid-off coal miner who went directly from high school into his or her career to be rapidly retrained in other, even unrelated, sectors without requiring two or four years of higher education. This increased efficiency means that job training (or re-training) is no longer cost-prohibitive, especially for older or less formally-educated workers. This is critically important in states like West Virginia where workers have struggled to transition their skillsets into other fields in the midst of a decline in traditional sectors such as mining and manufacturing.

As referenced in our written testimony to this committee on November 16, 2016, Augmented Reality (AR) work instructions have been shown to improve accuracy, speed, focus and worker satisfaction when utilized in the training and operation of complex manufacturing tasks through visual, step-by-step work instructions overlaid directly on top of components to be assembled.[7] In addition to shorter task completion times and less assembly errors, the visual and spatial nature of AR enables a lower total task load and a reduction in the learning curve of novice assemblers, while increasing task performance relevant to working memory.[8] Compared with video-based work instructions, AR produces a significantly reduced number of errors and scores better in terms of time and overall mental workload.[9]

Today, the majority of learning experiences occur out of context. Classroom training, online training modules, and online synchronous training are all variations of didactic content presentation. Augmented reality will provide learning professionals opportunities to engage students and trainees with scalable and effective mecha-

---

[1] Hou, Lei, *et al.*, "Using animated augmented reality to cognitively guide assembly." *Journal of Computing in Civil Engineering* 27.5 (2013): 439–451.

[2] F. Loch, F. Quint and I. Brishtel, "Comparing Video and Augmented Reality Assistance in Manual Assembly," *2016 12th International Conference on Intelligent Environments (IE)*, London, 2016, pp. 147–150.

[3] Henderson, S. J.; Feiner, S. 2009. "Evaluating the benefits of augmented reality for task localization in maintenance of an armored personnel carrier turret." International Symposium on Mixed and Augmented Reality, 2009 (ISMAR 2009). pp 135-144. Orlando, Florida.

[4] Caudell, T P and Mizell, D W 1992, Augmented reality: An application of heads-up display technology to manual manufacturing processes. Proc. Ieee Hawaii International Conf. on Systems Sciences, 1992.

[5] Webster, Anthony, *et al.*, "Augmented reality in architectural construction, inspection and renovation." *Proc. ASCE Third Congress on Computing in Civil Engineering.* 1996.

[6] K. Abhari *et al.*, "Training for Planning Tumour Resection: Augmented Reality and Human Factors," in *IEEE Transactions on Biomedical Engineering*, vol. 62, no. 6, pp. 1466–1477, June 2015.

[7] Fusing Self-Reported and Sensor Data from Mixed-Reality Training, *(I/ITSEC) 2014, Trevor Richardson, Stephen Gilbert, Joseph Holub, Frederick Thompson, Anastacia MacAllister, Rafael Radkowski, Eliot Winer Iowa State University, Paul Davies, Scott Terry, The Boeing Company.*

[8] Hou, Lei, *et al., ibid.*

[9] F. Loch, F. Quint and I. Brishtel. *ibid.*

nisms to practice new skills in a hands-on manner, while still being supported by digital tools. This is especially valuable for workers who may not have seen a college or vocational classroom in more than twenty years, if at all.

How does AR improve the speed of knowledge-transfer and improve its retention? A key element is AR's ability to combine the real-world environment with digital information. When it comes to learning new concepts and skills, no training method beats hands-on experience. Experiencing the consequences of success and failure in real time helps us make neural connections that are much stronger and longer lasting than simply consuming content. Wearable head-up displays with AR capabilities give the wearer a view that fuses the complexity and messiness of the real world with the precision and reliability of a digital display, providing access to the real-world scene for the hands-on aspect of training, while enhancing it with didactic or reference information to keep us on track. It is notably effective in enhancing spatial reasoning.

II. Enhancing the overall job climate

At a macroeconomic level, Augmented Reality can enhance the job climate by increasing productivity, which increases demand, which then increases employment. For example, Augmented Reality is likely to increase demand for manufacturing jobs due to its ability to directly improve manufacturing productivity. Studies show that Augmented Reality technology delivers significant improvements in worker productivity in the context of manufacturing and assembly.[10] This higher growth in manufacturing productivity, however, does not lead to a decline in employment. According to empirical research conducted by Yale Economics Professor William Nordhaus, the evidence shows that "rapid productivity growth leads to increased rather than decreased employment in manufacturing," as increased productivity leads to lower prices, thereby expanding demand, which results in increased employment.[11]

III. Augmented reality applications for rural areas

Of course, even if increased demand for manufactured goods results in increased manufacturing employment, those jobs may be unavailable in some areas, especially in rural states, if there are few or no factories located there. But far from leaving rural communities behind, some of the strongest use cases for Augmented Reality (AR) are specifically tailored to rural industries. As several senators have an interest in this topic, we have prepared the following discussion on AR applications in agriculture and forestry.

i. Augmented Reality and Smart Agriculture

State-of-the-art farm management practices such as precision agriculture, site specific crop management, and Internet of Things (IoT) farming have reduced costs and improved yields for farmers around the world. Augmented Reality (AR) applications can enhance many aspects of smart agriculture by providing tools that streamline the measurement and collection of inputs, and the delivery of analysis and insights that enable data-driven decision making.

IoT smart agriculture is one of the driving forces that allows the United States to produce 7,637 kilograms of cereal per hectare, nearly twice the world average in crop yield.[12] A wide range of sensors are now being implemented: BI Intelligence predicts that IoT device installations in the agriculture world will increase from 30 million in 2015 to 75 million in 2020, a compound annual growth rate of 20 percent.[13]

Thanks in part to the steady reduction in electronics and data storage costs, a wide range of sensors are being utilized across smart agriculture including biological, chemical and gas analyzers, water sensors, meteorological sensors, weed seekers, optical cameras, Light Detection and Ranging (LIDAR), photometric sensors, soil respiration, photosynthesis sensors, Leaf Area Index (LAI) sensors, range finders, Dendrometers, and hygrometers. Whether in unmanned aerial or ground vehicles (UAVs or UGVs), or stationed in the field, these IoT sensors sample, measure and collect key performance data including soil fertility diagnostics, yield as-planted,

---

[10] Hou, Lei, *et al., ibid.*

[11] Nordhaus, W. *The Sources of the Productivity Rebound and the Manufacturing Employment.* National Bureau of Economic Research, Working Paper No. 11354 May 2005. JEL No. O4, E1

[12] Cereal yield (kg per hectare). The World Bank. Accessed from: *http://data.worldbank.org/ indicator/AG.YLD.CREL.KG.* Accessed 12/18/16.

[13] Meola, Andrew. "Why IoT, Big Data & Smart Farming is the Future of Agriculture." *Business Insider.* October 7, 2016. Accessed from: *http://www.businessinsider.com/internet-of-things-smart-agriculture-2016–10.* Accessed 12/18/16.

and as-applied, and water utilization. AR technology could provide additional insights into the optimization of seed, fertilizer, and chemical input, planting prescriptions, profit mapping and analysis and future crop planning.

An AR interface displayed within devices such as the DAQRI Smart Helmet can show this vital information contextually within individual management zones, with real-time data like soil moisture levels, sunlight cations, projected Nitrogen use, and other advanced analytics appearing in the wearable device's view as the farmer traverses the ground.

Augmented reality systems have been proposed for agricultural uses across the spectrum including insect identification and pest management,[14] damage level estimation of diseased plant leaves,[15] outdoor visualization of agricultural geographic information system (GIS) data,[16] and GPS guidance for agricultural tractors.[17] Additional use cases might include visualizing prescriptive planning, enabling data collection of variables such as crop yield, terrain features and topography, organic matter content, moisture levels, nitrogen levels, pH, soil electrical conductivity, magnesium, and potassium.

Many other data visualization use cases that improve decision making in real-time could be implemented, for example three-dimensional on-site visualization of topographic maps and geomatic data such as altitude, expected crop yield and actual crop yield.[18]

It is well within the capabilities of AR technology to provide farmers push notifications, with a farmer looking out over the field and red warning notifications popping up where weed, insect, disease or drought pressures pass a given threshold.

Congress and the Administration, whether through the U.S. Department of Agriculture or other Federal agencies, should provide seed money and other grants to set up field studies in this area to document the outcomes and determine how much benefit the farming community may derive from these agricultural applications of AR technology.

ii. Augmented Reality Farm Equipment Repair & Maintenance

Augmented Reality can enhance farm operations by providing ways to improve outcomes and increase efficiency in training, maintenance, repair, and part ordering of farm machinery and equipment. Similar applications of AR as a facilitator in the maintenance of aircraft have resulted in better learning and recall, improving knowledge-transfer and training outcomes.[19] This same use of AR for airplanes can be applied to farm equipment to help farm managers monitor machine analytics, anticipate problems and analyze breakdowns quickly, reducing downtime and helping to keep planting and harvest on schedule. Moreover, this technology shows potential in reducing overall use of pesticides while targeting problem areas. It may also reduce farmers' trips to the field thanks to the increased connectedness it provides.

iii. Augmented Reality Applications in Forestry

In forestry—another key rural industry—smart IoT techniques are being utilized with the aim of controlling parameters of interest such as diameter of trees, crown height, bark thickness and other variables, such as canopy, humidity, illumination, and CO_2 transformation.

The application of wearables in forestry can be used in identifying and managing tree populations utilizing the same parameters as used in individual management zones with AR in Farming. In addition, wearables could provide first rate field training for students and new employees in real-time tree identification and other relevant facts.

---

[14] A. Nigam, P. Kabra and P. Doke, "Augmented Reality in agriculture," *2011 IEEE 7th International Conference on Wireless and Mobile Computing, Networking and Communications (WiMob),* Wuhan, 2011, pp. 445–448.

[15] S. Prasad, S. K. Peddoju and D. Ghosh, "Mobile Mixed Reality Based Damage Level Estimation of Diseased Plant Leaf," *2014 Eighth International Conference on Next Generation Mobile Apps, Services and Technologies,* Oxford, 2014, pp. 72–77.

[16] G. R. King, W. Piekarski and B. H. Thomas, "ARVino—outdoor augmented reality visualisation of viticulture GIS data," *Fourth IEEE and ACM International Symposium on Mixed and Augmented Reality (ISMAR'05),* 2005, pp. 52–55.

[17] Santana-Fernández, Javier; Gómez-Gil, Jaime; Del-Pozo-San-Cirilo, Laura. 2010. "Design and Implementation of a GPS Guidance System for Agricultural Tractors Using Augmented Reality Technology." *Sensors* 10, no. 11: 10435–10447.

[18] Goddard, Ted. "Augmented Reality Farming Geomatics." Accessed from: *https://www.youtube.com/watch?v=qrZYb5aa44k.* Accessed on 12/16/16.

[19] Valimont, R. B., Gangadharan, S. N., Vincenzi, D. A., & Majoros, A. E. (2007). The Effectiveness of Augmented Reality as a Facilitator of Information Acquisition in Aviation Maintenance Applications. Journal of Aviation/Aerospace Education & Research, 16(2). Retrieved from *http://commons.erau.edu/jaaer/vol16/iss2/9.*

IV. Augmented Reality Applications in Mining

In addition to these examples of Augmented Reality (AR) applications in rural areas, there are excellent use cases for AR in mining. Increased access to relevant real-time information saves time for workers and improves decision-making. This is one of the key benefits that AR can provide to mine workers.

Pervasive sensing—the practice of deploying large numbers of sensors and linking them to communication networks in order to analyze their collective data—is already being used in the mining industry to support remote operations, health and safety, and exploration and mapping. The identification and management of ore grade, which is relevant across all stages of the mining process, can be provided by sensing technologies during exploration, extraction, haulage and processing activities.[20] AR has been proposed as a mechanism to visualize sub-surface mining data,[21] and beyond that depth and localization data, 3D ranging and mapping, infrared data, and machine condition monitoring data are all examples of information that can be displayed in context to workers onsite using Augmented Reality head-up displays in order to improve operational efficiency and safety.

Augmented Reality can also help reduce mining accidents and lost workers. Major safety issues in the mining industry occur when personnel are in the field, such as when workers get lost underground and can no longer find their way back to the surface, or when miners encounter dangerous or explosive gases. Wearable AR devices have the additional added benefit of providing worker localization, allowing teams to remain in contact when miners lose visual contact with their teammates, and enabling the rapid localization of workers when emergency attention is needed.

———

RESPONSE TO WRITTEN QUESTION SUBMITTED BY HON. JOHN THUNE TO
STANLEY PIERRE-LOUIS

Question. As the potential applications for augmented reality grow, it is important to address cybersecurity risks to consumer and business information and computer generated visuals. How can companies use existing, voluntary guidance on best practices, such as those from the National Institute of Standards and Technology, and enhanced cyber-threat information sharing to assist in cybersecurity efforts?

Answer. Developers of augmented and mixed reality products and services rely on common communications tools and networks. These include, among other things, personal computers, mobile and other handheld devices, video game consoles, communications networks, servers and various types of network-connected storage. Like their peers, developers of augmented and mixed reality products and services must assess potential vulnerabilities in order to defend their systems, products and information from threats posed by malicious actors.

The National Institute of Standards and Technology's ("NIST") voluntary cybersecurity framework serves as a critical tool for any organization looking to establish and/or improve its procedures for assessing, managing and reducing cybersecurity risk. Although the NIST framework focuses on protecting critical infrastructure, such as transportation, water and communications systems, several of its priorities apply more broadly, including:

- protecting, defending and securing information infrastructure and digital networks;
- innovating and accelerating investment for the security and growth of digital networks and the digital economy;
- enhancing cybersecurity workforce capabilities; and
- ensuring an open, fair, competitive and secure global digital economy for companies and consumers alike.[1]

The NIST framework provides a coherent baseline for corporate cybersecurity management programs and has the added benefit of being easy to understand by nontechnical professionals. Its design can help organizations craft a cybersecurity program or improve an existing one. It creates a common language for organizations to understand their cybersecurity posture, set goals for cybersecurity improvements,

---

[20] M. E. Kiziroglou; D. E. Boyle; E. M. Yeatman; J. J. Cilliers, "Opportunities for sensing systems in mining," in *IEEE Transactions on Industrial Informatics*, vol.PP, no.99, pp.1–1.

[21] Roberts, Gethin W., *et al.,* "The use of augmented reality, GPS and INS for subsurface data visualization." FIG XXII International Congress. 2002. APA

[1] Commission on Enhancing National Cybersecurity, Report on Securing and Growing the Digital Economy (Dec. 1, 2016), *https://www.nist.gov/document/cybersecurity-commission-report-final-postpdf.*

monitor their progress and foster communications internally and externally. Stakeholders should continue to improve upon this framework, but adoption should remain voluntary based on the individual needs of each organization.

Companies can also avail themselves of other resources offered by Federal agencies, including automated alerts published by NIST, the United States Computer Emergency Readiness Team ("US–CERT") and the Federal Bureau of Investigation ("FBI"), all of which serve as key resources regarding security threats, incidents, vulnerabilities and even critical software updates.

In addition, the Cybersecurity Information Sharing Act of 2015, along with the creation of Information Sharing and Analysis Organizations, will likely facilitate the dissemination of critical information regarding cybersecurity threats and defensive measures.

————

RESPONSE TO WRITTEN QUESTIONS SUBMITTED BY HON. MARCO RUBIO TO
STANLEY PIERRE-LOUIS

Question 1. As we conduct our oversight role as lawmakers, how can we ensure that technology start-ups, like Magic Leap, are able to continue to advance in the 21st century economy without imposing unnecessary red tape?

Answer. Succeeding in the digital economy depends largely on access to talent, capital and consumers. The government can assist that effort by minimizing restrictions on each of these components, thereby reducing barriers to markets—especially for start-ups and other small businesses.

Access to talent requires a workforce equipped to innovate. For the video game industry, special emphasis is placed on candidates steeped in STEM (Science, Technology, Engineering and Mathematics) and STEAM (STEM + Arts) education as video games require both technology and content creation skillsets. Smarter investment in education and in job training programs would serve to bolster the pipeline for a workforce in the tech and creative content sectors.

Access to capital requires incentive-based market conditions created by policies that encourage investment. At the Federal level, this means adopting tax policies that spur economic activity for business and eliminating regulations that restrain economic growth opportunities.

Access to consumers requires a state-of-the-art, networked and secure infrastructure available in all regions of the country. Broader broadband deployment in both metropolitan and rural areas would create new opportunities to reach consumers where they are and widen consumer offerings.

For start-ups, the success factors outlined above are all the more critical. Magic Leap, for example, launched in 2010 in a region not traditionally known for tech start-ups (Ft. Lauderdale, FL). Nonetheless, it has attracted more than 800 employees and raised more than $1.4B in investment capital to work towards its mission to create a new technology platform. That platform has the potential to transform applications in fields as varied as entertainment, medicine and engineering. Regulating its future before it has the opportunity to come to market would undercut American entrepreneurial initiative and technological innovation at a critical juncture.

Question 2. In your opinion, would current regulations placed on the gaming and computer industry be appropriate to apply to this new generation technology?

Answer. Federal laws and regulations covering the video game and computer industries, such as privacy and data security, have proven to be sufficiently robust to protect consumer interests while remaining flexible enough to allow industries to innovate and deliver products and services to customers specified to their needs. Moreover, in each state and territory, laws governing negligence, trespass, privacy, data protection and product liability are commonplace. In short, today's legal framework should prove sufficient and adaptable to cover new technologies like augmented and mixed reality.

ESA's members are committed to meaningful privacy and data security protections. A hallmark of the video game industry remains its creation of a voluntary program that educates consumers about the content they purchase. As noted in our earlier testimony, in 1994, the video game industry launched the Entertainment Software Rating Board ("ESRB"), a non-profit, self-regulatory body that assigns ratings for video games and apps so parents can make informed choices. The ESRB rating system encompasses guidance about age-appropriateness, content and interactive elements. The Federal Trade Commission ("FTC") has repeatedly praised the effectiveness of the ESRB rating system, our industry's compliance with the system and its acceptance among parents.[2] Notwithstanding this support, several states passed "harmful to minors" legislation seeking to stop the sale of certain games. In 2011, however, the U.S. Supreme Court recognized in Brown v. Entertainment Merchants Association that video games are expressive works that enjoy the same First Amendment protections as "books, plays, and movies." [3] In an opinion by the late Justice Antonin Scalia, the Supreme Court rejected the argument that "video games present special problems" because they are "interactive," noting that "interactivity" has always been the goal of expressive works: "the better it is, the more interactive." [4]

The Supreme Court left little doubt that our foundational laws governing speech are well-equipped to address emerging technologies like augmented and mixed reality. Still, threats to First Amendment and other freedoms may arise as new products and experiences come to market. Instead, government should encourage industry to continue to foster voluntary, self-regulatory programs that create awareness while seeking to secure consumer adoption.

Question 3. Autism is an issue I feel very passionate about and have worked on going back to my time in the Florida legislature. Some have suggested that augmented reality games can benefit people on the autism spectrum in terms of getting them out of the house and developing their social skills. Is the industry doing any of its own scientific research to determine the actual benefits of augmented gaming to people on the autism spectrum?

Answer. We applaud your commitment to improving the lives of those living with autism spectrum disorders.

Medical research continues to improve the diagnosis, prevention and treatment of autism and its associated medical conditions. As your question suggests, the use of augmented reality and GPS location-based games have been used to encourage those on the autism spectrum to explore their surroundings and develop social interaction skills.[5] According to an educator who has conducted studies on the use of computer games to address autism, the visual stimuli in certain games improve the learning process for autistic persons.[6] Other researchers have noted that the social nature certain games helps increase sensory input, build family bonds, promote social acceptance and inclusion, encourage reciprocal conversations and create a sense of accomplishment.[7]

More broadly, medical researchers have employed augmented reality games to enhance social interaction and hand-eye coordination in children with autism. These researchers found that the games appeared to help ease the patients into becoming more comfortable around unfamiliar people.[8] They also observed that these games appeared to improve concentration and imagination because of their repetitive movement and visual feedback. In addition, some researchers believe that aug-

---

[2] See FTC Undercover Shopper Survey on Entertainment Ratings Enforcement Finds Compliance Highest among Video Game Sellers and Movie Theaters (March 25, 2013), *https://www.ftc.gov/news-events/pressreleases/2013/03/ftc-undercover-shopper-survey-entertainment-ratings-enforcement;* FTC, Marketing Violent Entertainment to Children, 28, 30 (Dec. 2009), *https://www.ftc.gov/reports/marketing-violent-entertainmentchildren-sixth-follow-review-industry-practices-motion;* and FTC, Marketing Violent Entertainment to Children, 27, 29, C–18, (April 2007), *https://www.ftc.gov/reports/marketing-violent-entertainment-children-fifth-follow-reviewindustry-practices-motion.*

[3] 564 U.S. 786, 790 (2011).

[4] *Id.* at 798.

[5] While some medical professionals and researchers have made use of certain video games to address autism, we are not aware of any video game developers making claims that gameplay provides medical benefits to autism patients.

[6] Samantha Finch, "Pokémon Go" & Autism: Augmented Reality Game's Success in Getting Autistic Children Out Of Their Comfort Zone, Parent Herald (July 18, 2016), *http://www.parentherald.com/articles/55253/20160718/pok%C3%A9mon-go-autism-augmented-reality-game-s-success-getting-autistic.htm.*

[7] Malinda Robedeau, Pokémon Go: Life Changing Benefits for those with Autism, GT Independence (Aug. 23, 2016), *https://www.gtindependence.com/pokemon-go-life-changing-benefits-for-those-with-autism/.*

[8] S.K. Bhatt, *et al.,* Augmented Reality Game Therapy for Children with Autism Spectrum Disorder, Int'l Journal on Smart Sensing and Intelligent Systems, Vol. 7, No. 2 (March 2014), *www.s2is.org/Issues/v7/n2/papers/paper5.pdf;* see also Laura Bartoli, *et al.,* Exploring Motion-Based Touchless Games for Autistic Children's Learning, ACM (June 2013), *www.associazioneastrolabio.it/wp-content/uploads/2014/04/Articolo-New-York.pdf;* see also Lizbeth Escobedo, *et al.,* Using Augmented Reality to Help Children with Autism Stay Focused, IEEE Pervasive Computing (Jan. 2014), *https://www.researchgate.net/publication/260526735 ▮ Using ▮ Augmented ▮ Reality ▮ to ▮ Help ▮ Children ▮ with ▮ Autism ▮ Stay ▮ Focused.*

mented reality games may improve the ability of those with autism to read social cues and learn to pretend play.[9]

As mentioned in earlier testimony, Microsoft is already selling its mixed reality visor, called HoloLens, to developers. Applications under development include several business, engineering and architectural projects. In the health field, uses of HoloLens include:

- assisting medical students with anatomy curriculum at Case Western's medical schools;[10]
- early testing by Duke University doctors to assist with brain surgery;[11]
- use by spinal surgeons in Brazil to perform more accurate spinal fusions;[12] and
- enabling medical students to practice abdominal examinations with a physical simulator before facing real patients.[13]

Applications of HoloLens to address autism have yet to occur. However, researchers at the Lakeside Center for Autism (Washington) as well as at the College of Staten Island (New York) have begun to employ a motion-based technology developed by Microsoft, known as Kinect, to study whether its use can improve the lives of autistic children by encouraging physical and educational activities.[14]

Question 4. What would you say our high schools and universities can be doing better in the coming years to ensure that people in Florida and in the United States acquire the skills and preparation to fill these jobs?

Answer. As noted above, jobs in the digital economy will increasingly rely on STEM and STEAM skillsets. For students, this may mean placing more emphasis on coding, engineering and other computer-related coursework. For those already in the workforce who need to transition to a job in a technology field (particularly in rural areas), this may mean acquiring new skills through re-training programs. Augmented and mixed reality technologies promise to play a role in both scenarios.

For its part, the video game industry has worked diligently to encourage educational initiatives that expand opportunities in the digital economy, including through:

- the National STEM Video Game Challenge, an annual game design competition that challenges students and developers to create original games that stimulate interest in science, technology, engineering and math learning;[15]
- the ESA LOFT (Leaders on the Fast Track) Video Game Innovation Fellows program, which, in collaboration with the Hispanic Heritage Foundation (HHF), encourages minorities ages 15–25 to create original video games and apps to address social issues in their communities;[16] and
- the ESA Foundation, which awards scholarships to the next generation of industry innovators and supports charitable organizations and schools that leverage entertainment software and technology to create meaningful opportunities for America's youth.[17]

---

[9] Olivia Reese, Autism and Google Glass: Augmented Reality Headwear Teaches Autistic People To Read Social Cues & Emotions, Parent Herald (Sept. 23, 2016), *http://www.parent herald.com/articles/68752/20160923/autism-googleglass-augmented-reality-headwear-teaches-autistic-people-read.htm;* see also Monica Rozenfeld, Augmented Reality Can Help Children With Autism Tap Into Their Imaginations, The Institute (April 1, 2015), *http://theinstitute.ieee.org/technology-topics/consumer-electronics/augmented-reality-can-help-children-withautism-tap-into-their-imaginations.*

[10] Kathryn Jeffords, Virtual and Augmented Reality: Changing the Game in Healthcare, Science Media Awards Summit in the Hub (June 29, 2016), *www.s2is.org/Issues/v7/n2/papers/paper5.pdf.*

[11] Laurent Giret, Doctors at Duke University are Testing HoloLens Assisted Brain Surgery, OnMSFT (October 2016), *https://www.onmsft.com/news/doctors-at-duke-university-are-testing-hololens-assisted-brain-surgery.*

[12] Megan Wood, Kathryn Jeffords, Brazilian Surgeons Utilize Microsoft's HoloLens for Spinal Fusions: 5 Highlights, Becker's Spine Review (Dec. 5, 2016), *http://www.beckersspine.com/orthopedic-a-spine-device-a-implantnews/item/34413-brazilian-surgeons-utilize-microsoft-s-hololens-for-spinal-fusions-5-highlights.html.*

[13] See Medical Simulation demonstration, *https://www.youtube.com/watch?v=JGiVVObY0Ew.*

[14] See Lakeside Center for Autism demonstration, *https://www.youtube.com/watch?v=uuP6 d42hK8k;* see College of Staten Island demonstration, *http://www.playfitness.com/autism-research-project-edu.*

[15] See *http://stemchallenge.org/featured/national-stem-video-game-challenge-launches-fifth-competition/.*

[16] See *http://www.loftcsl.org/esa ▌ loft ▌ fellowship.*

[17] See *http://www.esafoundation.org/.*

Our industry has also partnered with the U.S. Department of Education to create ED Games Day, which entails a mini-conference that highlights video games created as tools for learning as well as a "game jam" and research presentations on educational games.[18] In addition, ESA has sponsored education-related events at E3, its annual industry expo.[19] And, ESA works with EverFi, an education technology innovator, on the ESA Digital Living Project, which combines the power of cutting-edge instructional design, rich media, online video games and real world simulations to educate middle school and high school students about technology, digital literacy and career opportunities in STEM fields. Since the program's inception, the ESA Digital Living Project has reached nearly 20,000 students across three states.[20]

We look forward to continued work with educators to help prepare students for the next wave of opportunities made possible by these technologies.

Question 5. What message would you like to send to educators and students alike about the industry's future and the opportunities it presents?

Answer. The video game industry sits at the intersection of creativity and innovation. We bring together the best minds in interactive content development and technology to entertain audiences around the world. Our industry also has proven to be a strong engine for economic growth. In 2015, the industry generated more than $23.5 billion in revenue in the United States, and it directly and indirectly employed more than 146,000 people.[21] Also in 2015, there were 1,641 video game companies in the United States, including 60 in Florida, where games like NFL Madden 17 by EA Sports are made.[22] Moreover, the average compensation for a video game industry employee was nearly $95,000.[23] In addition, some 406 U.S. colleges and universities had video game design programs in 2015, including at least 20 in Florida.[24] In short, the video game industry remains on a growth trajectory, creating a never-ending quest to recruit the best and brightest.

However, national statistics regarding digital literacy have highlighted the need to provide more STEM and STEAM education around the country. In 2015, of the nearly 3.8 million ninth graders in the country, only six percent were expected to choose a STEM-focused degree in college.[25] Video games may prove crucial to attracting and retaining students in STEM and STEAM fields.[26] In fact, a recent study found that combining video games with other subjects, including those in the STEM and STEAM fields, doubled the amount of women in those educational programs and boasted an 88 percent retention rate.[27]

We encourage educators to embrace STEM and technology education opportunities, leverage technology in a safe and effective manner and create active pathways for career success in STEM, STEAM and other related fields.

---

[18] See *http://blog.ed.gov/2016/01/ed-games-day-comes-to-washington-d-c/*.

[19] Tony Wan, Video Game Industry Gives Education a Reboot at E3 2015, EdSurge News (June 21, 2015), *https://www.edsurge.com/news/2015-06-21-video-game-industry-gives-education-a-reboot-at-e3-2015*.

[20] See *info.everfi.com/rs/everfi/images/ESA▮PressRelease▮May%2019▮FINAL.pdf* (May 19, 2014).

[21] See ESA 2015 Annual Report, *http://www.theesa.com/wp-content/uploads/2016/04/ESA-Annual-Report-20151.pdf*, and Video Games in the 21st Century, The 2014 Report, *http://www.theesa.com/wp-content/uploads/2014/11/VideoGames21stCentury▮2014.pdf*.

[22] See *http://www.theesa.com/article/new-research-underscores-breadth-and-vibrancy-of-u-s-video-game-industry/*; see also *http://www.theesa.com/about-esa/courses-certificates-degree-programs/*.

[23] See Video Games in the 21st Century, The 2014 Report, *http://www.theesa.com/wp-content/uploads/2014/11/VideoGames21stCentury▮2014.pdf*. Overall, the average annual 2015 compensation paid to core copyright workers is $93,221, which far exceeds the average annual compensation paid to all U.S. workers—$67,715—amounting to a 38 percent "compensation premium" over the average U.S. annual wage. See *http://www.iipawebsite.com/pdf/2016CpyrtRpt Full.PDF*.

[24] See *http://www.theesa.com/about-esa/courses-certificates-degree-programs/*. In fact, the Princeton Review ranks three Florida universities among the "Top 25 Graduate Schools to Study Game Design for 2016," including the University of Miami. See *https://www.princeton review.com/press/game-design-press-release*.

[25] See ESA 2015 Annual Report, *http://www.theesa.com/wp-content/uploads/2016/04/ESA-Annual-Report-20151.pdf*.

[26] Jessica Trybus, Game-Based Learning: What it is, Why it Works, and Where it's Going, New Media Institute (2014), *http://www.newmedia.org/game-based-learning—what-it-is-why-it-works-and-where-its-going.html*.

[27] Rich Taylor, Opportunities to Learn, Work With Video Games Multiply, Huffington Post (Nov. 11, 2015), *http://www.huffingtonpost.com/rich-taylor/opportunities-to-learn-wo▮b▮8538 426.html*; see also Priming the Pump 2015: Higher Education Video Game Alliance Survey of Program Graduates (2015), *http://docplayer.net/5662014Priming-the-pump-2015-higher-education-video-game-alliance-survey-of-program-graduates.html*.

Question 6. The interface created by these new technologies can be a tremendous asset to the Department of Defense, especially for training. How can the Department of Defense collaborate with innovators to push the limits of mixed reality technologies to ensure our men and women in uniform continue to be the best trained and equipped fighting force on this Earth?

Answer. The military has made extensive use of augmented and mixed reality technologies for training and battlefield operations.

In training, augmented and mixed reality technologies have been used to improve upon conventional methods by providing more a realistic, immersive experience for the trainees while reducing costs for the military.[28] These technologies simulate real-life environments, targets and threat situations, whether in flight, at sea or on the ground. They enable the military to train on scenarios that are too difficult, dangerous and/or costly to practice in the field or even in a conventional simulation.[29] These technologies also make learning more effective by providing the option of training scenarios at multiple levels of difficulty.[30] And, they can train soldiers on the capabilities and maintenance of vehicles and other equipment under various conditions.[31]

In combat, augmented and mixed reality technologies have the potential to address innumerable challenges. For example, using augmented reality visors, a soldier can have data superimposed in her field of view in real time, thereby maintaining her gaze on the battlefield while processing the information rather than by looking down at a phone or a laptop.[32] Soldiers and intelligence centers can share real-time updates on battlefield conditions, geo-location of allies and target coordinates.[33] These technologies can also provide immersive functionality, like "X-ray vision," which enables the soldier to see an object (*e.g.,* an enemy) that is obstructed by another object (*e.g.,* wreckage).[34] And, these technologies can serve a filtering function by using algorithms to limit the quantity and type of information displayed to each user.[35]

Growing the potential applications of augmented and mixed reality technologies for military readiness will require an investment in research and talent development.

Question 7. Much of the attention towards augmented, virtual, and mixed reality technologies have been devoted towards gaming and entertainment purposes. I believe companies such as Magic Leap and Microsoft have good reasons to be focusing on the business application for this interface. Can you elaborate on how such technology platforms could help increase productivity in the workplace or increase learning and proficiency for students?

Answer. The video game industry's use of augmented and mixed reality technologies will focus primarily on engaging audiences to entertainment them. However, other uses of these technology platforms appear ripe for enhancing workplace productivity and classroom learning.

In the workplace, emerging business applications include heads-up displays in manufacturing systems to support complex production processes, collaborative product design and prototyping; remote assistance from engineers and technicians; medical systems that enable surgeons to access relevant data during surgery without being distracted; and education and training.[36] Experts predict that the business applications of these technologies will multiply exponentially as more businesses begin

---

[28] See Augmented Reality, U.S. Naval Research Laboratory, *https://www.nrl.navy.mil/itd/ imda/research/5581/augmented-reality.*

[29] Oliver Baus, *et al.,* Moving from Virtual Reality Exposure-Based Therapy to Augmented Reality Exposure-Based Therapy: A Review, Frontiers in Human Neuroscience (March 4, 2014), *http://journal.frontiersin.org/article/10.3389/fnhum.2014.00112/full.*

[30] *Id.*

[31] Sabine Webel, *et al.,* An Augmented Reality Training Platform for Assembly and Maintenance Skills, Robotics and Autonomous Systems, Vol. 61, Issue 4 (April 2013) at pp. 398–403, *http://www.sciencedirect.com/science/article/pii/S0921889012001674.*

[32] Andrew Rosenblum, Augmented Reality Glasses are Coming to the Battlefield, Popular Science (April 22, 2015), *http://www.popsci.com/experimental-ar-glasses-offer-marines-hands-free-intel.*

[33] *Id.*

[34] See Augmented Reality, U.S. Naval Research Laboratory, *https://www.nrl.navy.mil/itd/ imda/research/5581/augmented-reality.*

[35] *Id.*

[36] See AR and Wearable Tech is a Marriage Made for the Enterprise says Beecham Research (Jan. 20, 2016), *http://www.realwire.com/releases/AR-and-wearable-tech-is-a-marriage-made-for-the-enterprise-says-Beecham.*

to adopt them.[37] In fact, some think that these technologies will entirely change the way we do business. For example, collaboration among remote employees could become seamless; with augmented reality and mixed reality, it could be as if every employee were in the same room and able to write on the same white board. Employee training could be transformed from a one-dimensional experience to a completely immersive one, in which the employee can practice a task in a simulated, real-world setting.[38] In fact, Microsoft is working with educational publisher *Pear- son* to use the HoloLens to create a number of learning tools, including online tutor- ing and coaching in areas as disparate as nursing, engineering and construction.[39] Augmented and mixed reality technologies are similarly valuable in the classroom setting. The most visceral advantage is the immersive, interactive nature of these technologies. According to a leading professor of education, "[r]esearch shows that interacting with [augmented reality] alone improves students' understanding of a concept." [40] Use of this technology can transform the abstract into something real and tangible that a student can see, hear and with which the student can interact.[41]

RESPONSE TO WRITTEN QUESTION SUBMITTED BY HON. JOE MANCHIN TO STANLEY PIERRE-LOUIS

Question. As a former Governor and in my role as a United States Senator, I have remained committed to enhancing the job climate in my state so that West Virginians have good paying jobs and the skills to compete in the global economy. Part of this job growth is going to come from the technology sector. We are beginning to see an uptick in technology startups in different parts of the state, but I believe there are opportunities for tools such as augmented reality to enhance workforce training.

The technological advancements of the 21st century should not leave rural communities behind, and as West Virginia continues to develop its technology sector and train its workforce: How can augmented reality be used to train workers in the digital economy?

Answer. In our written and oral testimony for the November 16, 2016, hearing on augmented and mixed reality before the U.S. Senate Committee on Commerce, Science, and Transportation, we highlighted how these technologies offer new ways for video game companies to create highly-expressive, immersive works for the purpose of entertaining our audiences. As described below, these technologies also enable applications that can benefit other industries and workers in rural communities.

Deploying augmented reality solutions can create impactful training programs that improve employee engagement, productivity and safety.[1] According to one research study, augmented reality "has matured to a point where organizations can use it as an internal tool to complement and enhance business processes, workflows and employee training." [2] Importantly, this is true not only of technology-based industries, but traditional industries as well.

For example, the agricultural sector has developed several uses of augmented reality to assist farmers with their work:

---

[37] Adam C. Uzialko, Augmented Reality Check: Innovative Ways Businesses are Embracing AR, Business News Daily (July 18, 2016), *http://www.businessnewsdaily.com/9245-augmented-reality-for-business.html.*

[38] *Id.*

[39] Mark Coppock, Microsoft and Pearson are partnering to Turn HoloLens into an Educational Tool, Digital Trends (Oct. 26, 2016), *http://www.digitaltrends.com/computing/pearson-hololens-mixed-reality-education/.*

[40] Susan A. Yoon, The Educator's Playbook: The Role of Augmented Reality in a Lesson Plan, Penn GSE Newsroom (2016), *http://www.gse.upenn.edu/news/educators-playbook/role-augmented-reality-lesson-plan.*

[41] Aaron Burch, The Top Ten Companies Working on Education in Virtual Reality and Augmented Reality, Touchstone Research (June 2, 2016), *https://touchstoneresearch.com/the-top-10-companies-working-on-education-in-virtualreality-and-augmented-reality/.*

[1] *See Augmented Reality: A New Workforce Mobilization Paradigm,* Cognizant (October 2015), *https://www.cognizant.com/InsightsWhitepapers/Augmented-Reality-A-New-Workforce-Mobilization-Paradigm-codex1434.pdf; see also* Tommy Hynes, *Is there a Place for Augmented Reality in the Workplace,* Equator HR, *http://www.equatorhr.com/blog/is-there-a-place-for-augmented-reality-in-the-workplace.*

[2] *See Gartner Says Augmented Reality Will Become an Important Workplace Tool,* Gartner (January 14, 2014), *http://www.gartner.com/newsroom/id/2649315.*

- Solutions have been developed to allow farmers to predict crop yield by using three-dimensional visualizations on mobile devices.[3]
- Augmented reality prototypes have been built to assist farmers in insect identification and pest management.[4]
- Equipment manufacturers are working on ways to use augmented reality to assist in equipment use and maintenance as well as to compile data to help farmers and other workers perform their daily tasks.[5] In fact, at a recent conference, the equipment manufacturer Caterpillar demonstrated how the use of Microsoft's mixed reality headset, known as HoloLens, could be used to help consumers visualize its vehicles.[6]

The mining sector has employed augmented reality to address worker training; improve safety and productivity; and adapt to skills shortages and worker turnover.[7] In the shipbuilding sector, augmented reality solutions are being developed to visually enhance worker training and access to information required for job performance, "including steps [for task completion], cautions, knowledge from expert workers, schematics and any other digitized data." [8] Through the use of this technology, a worker with a mobile device would have access to 3–D product models; planning and training for future work; step-by-step maintenance instructions; and safety information.[9] And in the aerospace sector, Lockheed Martin has collaborated on augmented reality projects to speed up the maintenance process for F–22 and F–35 fighter jets, such that "[w]hen an engineer looks at the aircraft using the smart glasses, they see digitally displayed plans projected over the physical plane," and "[t]hey can then use a tablet to enter any damage or defects." [10]

While augmented reality will serve an important role in training—and re-training—today's workforce, it promises to be equally important as a tool to prepare tomorrow's workforce for the competitive jobs landscape that awaits them. Experts have noted that augmented reality provides a more immersive, interactive means to teach students STEM (Science, Technology, Engineering and Mathematics) and STEAM (STEM + Arts) subjects.[11] In addition, a recent study found that programs that combine video game coursework with other subjects boasted an 88 percent retention rate.[12] In fact, video game design programs have served as successful means to attract and retain interest in STEM and STEAM careers more broadly.[13]

For its part, West Virginia boasts several programs that emphasize STEM and STEAM education. For example, several schools—including West Virginia University's Institute of Technology, Marshall University, Shephard University, Mountwest Community and Technical College, among others—offer programs or courses in

---

[3] *See Augmented Reality Farming*, ICEsoft Blog (July 16, 2013), *http://www.icesoft.org/blog/augmented-reality-farming/*; see also *https://www.youtube.com/watch?v=qrZYb5aa44k*.

[4] A. Nigam, *et al., Augmented Reality in Agriculture* (October 2011), *http://ieeexplore.ieee.org/document/6085361/*.

[5] See *https://www.youtube.com/watch?v=VGtCQWROytw*.

[6] John Callaham, *Microsoft HoloLens Can Bring a Caterpillar Loader from a Flat Catalog to a Full Size 3D Model*, (March 31, 2016), *http://www.windowscentral.com/microsoft-hololens-can-bring-caterpillar-loader-flat-catalog-full-size-3d-model*; see also *https://www.youtube.com/watch?v=e8AirvNicNs*.

[7] J. Bassan, *et al., The Augmented Mine Worker: Applications of Augmented Reality in Mining* (November 2011), *https://www.researchgate.net/profile/J∎Bassan/publication/274067824∎ The∎Augmented∎Mine∎Worker∎-∎Applications∎of∎Augmented∎Reality∎in∎Mining/links/5513d2120cf283ee083491d7.pdf;* F. Benes, *et al.,* Application of Augmented Reality in Mining Industry, SGEM (October 1, 2014), *http://sgem.org/sgemlib/spip.php?article4002.*

[8] G. Marshall, *Closing the Nation's Skills Gap*, Industry Week (January 13, 2016), *http://www.industryweek.com/education-training/closing-nations-skills-gap.*

[9] *Id.*

[10] *See Augmented Reality and Workplace Training*, SpongeUK (June 19, 2015), *http://spongeuk.com/2015/06/augmented-reality-and-workplace-training/*.

[11] *See, e.g.,* Susan A. Yoon, *The Educator's Playbook: The Role of Augmented Reality in a Lesson Plan*, Penn GSE Newsroom (2016), *http://www.gse.upenn.edu/news/educators-playbook/role-augmented-reality-lesson-plan* ("Research shows that interacting with [augmented reality] alone improves students' understanding of a concept.").

[12] Rich Taylor, *Opportunities to Learn, Work With Video Games Multiply*, Huffington Post (Nov. 11, 2015), *http://www.huffingtonpost.com/rich-taylor/opportunities-to-learn-wo∎b∎8538 426.html* (noting that the study also found that combining video games with other subjects also doubled the number of women in these educational programs); see also Priming the Pump 2015: Higher Education Video Game Alliance Survey of Program Graduates (2015), *http://docplayer.net/5662014-Priming-the-pump-2015-higher-education-video-game-alliance-survey-of-program-graduates.html.*

[13] Jessica Trybus, *Game-Based Learning: What it is, Why it Works, and Where it's Going*, New Media Institute (2014), *http://www.newmedia.org/game-based-learning—what-it-is-why-it-works-and-where-its-going.html.*

video game design.[14] In addition, the state has piloted programs like Globaloria to teach secondary education students coding, web design and game development skills.[15]

We encourage policymakers, educators and industry players alike to embrace technology education opportunities. By way of example, several Appalachian coal miners recently transitioned into coding careers through the work of an innovative company looking to tap into its local talent pool as a resource.[16] Workers in the digital economy will increasingly need to rely on STEM and STEAM skillsets, no matter where their jobs are located.

We appreciate the opportunity to participate in this important dialogue and stand ready to assist the Committee on its ongoing work in this area.

---

[14] In 2010, the *Princeton Review* ranked Marshall University's video game design program among the "Top 50 Undergraduate Schools to Study Game Design Programs." *See http:// www.marshall.edu/pressrelease.asp?ID=1935.*

[15] *See http://www.wvcpd.org/globaloria.aspx.*

[16] Erica Peterson, *From Coal To Code: A New Path For Laid-Off Miners In Kentucky,* NPR (May 6, 2016), *http://www.npr.org/sections/alltechconsidered/2016/05/06/477033781/from-coal-to-code-a-new-path-for-laid-off-miners-in-kentucky; see also* Tim Loh, *Appalachian Miners Are Learning to Code*(Feb. 2, 2016), *https://www.bloomberg.com/news/articles/2016–02–03/ from-coal-to-coding-appalachian-miners-getting-a-fresh-start.*

109

This page intentionally left blank.

110

This page intentionally left blank.

111

This page intentionally left blank.

www.ingramcontent.com/pod-product-compliance
Lightning Source LLC
Chambersburg PA
CBHW060158060326
40690CB00018B/4160